BOOK
7

WORDLY WISE
3OOO®

Direct Academic Vocabulary Instruction

Fourth Edition

Kenneth Hodkinson • Sandra Adams • Erika Hodkinson

EDUCATORS PUBLISHING SERVICE
Cambridge and Toronto

Editorial team: Carolyn Daniels, Marie Sweetman, Erika Wentworth
Cover Design: Deborah Rodman, Karen Swyers
Interior Design: Deborah Rodman

Vocabulary Extension Illustrations: Chris Murphy

Passage Illustrations for Lessons 2, 14, 17, 18: Q2AMedia

Passage Photograph Credits: Lesson 1: Rob Ferguson Jr; Lesson 3: Andrea Grossmann; Lesson 4: Charles Kaye/Fotolia; Lesson 5: HC/Fotolia; Lesson 6: Christopher Walker/Fotolia; Lesson 7: Durova; Lesson 8: Library of Congress Prints and Photographs Division Washington, D.C. 20540 USA; Lesson 9: Joser Pizarro/Fotolia; Lesson 10: Nicolas Larento/Fotolia; Lesson 11: Philippe Kurlapski; Lesson 12: Leeds City Art Gallery; Lesson 13: Library of Congress Prints and Photographs Division Washington, D.C. 20540 USA; Lesson 15: David Sytsma/Fotolia; Lesson 16: Toneteam/iStock.com via Getty Images; Lesson 19: Beatrice Preve/Fotolia; Lesson 20: Masterfile

Printed in Benton Harbor, MI, in June 2023
ISBN 978-0-8388-7707-4

7 8 9 10 PPG 26 25 24 23

Contents

Welcome to *Wordly Wise 3000*®

You've been learning words since you were a tiny baby. At first, you learned them only by hearing other people talk. Now that you are a reader, you have another way to learn words.

Obviously, it's important to know what words mean, but lots of times, we think we can get away without knowing some of them as we read. This could cause a problem. Say you are reading the directions for a new game. You know most of the words in the sentence you're reading. Then you stop for a word you don't recognize:

> *Please do not touch the* blegmy *or your score will be lost.*

You ask yourself, "What is a *blegmy?*" At first you think, "Well, it's only one word." But then you think, "What is it that I'm not supposed to touch?" All of a sudden, knowing what that one word means is important!

Clearly, the more words you know, the better your understanding of everything you read. *Wordly Wise 3000* will help you learn a lot of words, but it can't teach you *all* the words you'll ever need. It can, however, help guide your learning of new words on your own.

How Do You Learn What Words Mean?

There are two main ways you learn what words mean: directly and indirectly.

You have to learn some words *directly*. You may study them for a class, look them up in a dictionary or glossary, or ask someone what they mean. You also learn word meanings *indirectly* by hearing and reading the words. In fact, the more you listen and read, the more words you'll learn. Reading books, magazines, and online can help build your vocabulary.

At school, you learn a lot of words directly. If you're using this book, you are learning words directly. You are reading the words, learning what they mean, and studying them. Then you are practicing them as you do the activities. Finally, you might even use them in your own writing or conversations. There is an old saying: "Use a word three times and it's yours." Three times might not be enough, of course, but the idea is right. The more you practice using a word, the better you understand it.

What Is "School Language"?

School language—or school words—are the words you find in the books you read, from novels to textbooks, and on tests. You read them online as you look up information. Your teacher uses these words to explain an important concept about math or reading. Some have to do with a particular topic, such as the building of the Great Pyramid in Egypt. Others are words for tasks you are being asked to do, such as *summarize*. These words are different from the kinds of words you use when you're hanging out with your friends or talking casually with your family. That's why you often need to study such words directly. In this book, these important words are underlined to help you focus on them.

Wordly Wise 3000 is designed to teach you some of the words you need to do well in school and on tests—and later on in your jobs. It will also help you learn how to learn more words. Remember, there is no single thing that will help you understand what you read as much as knowing word meanings will.

How Do You Figure Out Word Meanings?

What should you do when you come to a word and you think you don't know what it means?

Say It

First, say it to yourself. Maybe once you do this, it will sound like a word you *do* know. Sometimes you know a word in your head without knowing what it looks like in print. So if you match up what you know and what you read—you have the word!

Use Context

If this doesn't work, take the next step: look at the context of the word—the other words and sentences around it. Sometimes these can give you a clue to the word's meaning. Here's an example:

Mr. Huerta had great respect for his opponent.

Say that you don't know what *opponent* means. Does Mr. Huerta have respect for his teacher? His mother? Then you read on:

> *The two players sat across from each other in the warm room. The chessboard was between them. Both looked as if they were concentrating very hard.*

Now you see that Mr. Huerta is taking part in a chess game. You know that in a chess game, one person plays another. So his *opponent* must be the person he is playing against. You reread the sentence using that meaning. Yes, that works. In this sentence, *opponent* means "someone you play against, or compete with."

Use Word Parts

If the context doesn't help, look at the parts of the word. Does it have any prefixes you know? How about suffixes? Or roots? These can help you figure out what it means. Look at this sentence:

> *Shania had the* misfortune *to hurt her arm right before the swim meet.*

If you don't know the meaning of *misfortune*, try looking at parts of the word. You might know that *fortune* means "luck." Maybe *mis-* is a prefix. You could look it up, or maybe you remember its meaning from studying prefixes in school. The prefix *mis-* means a few different things, but one of them is "bad." You try it out and reread the sentence using that meaning. It would certainly be bad luck, or a *misfortune,* to hurt your arm before a swim meet.

Look It Up

If saying the word or using context and word parts don't work, you can look it up in a dictionary—either a book or online reference—or a glossary.

Nobody knows the meaning of every word, but good readers know how to use these strategies to figure out words they don't know. Get into the habit of using them as you read, and you may be surprised at how automatic it becomes!

How Well Do You Know a Word?

It's important to know many words and to keep on learning more. But it's also important to know them well. In fact, some experts say that there are four levels of knowing a word:

1. I never saw/heard it before.
2. I've heard/seen it, but I don't know what it means.
3. I think it has something to do with…
4. I know it.*

Just because you can read a word and have memorized its definition, it doesn't mean that you know that word well. You want to know it so well that you know when to use it and when to use another word instead. One way to help deepen your knowledge of a word is to use a graphic organizer like the one below that tells about the word *portion*.

Concept of Definition Map

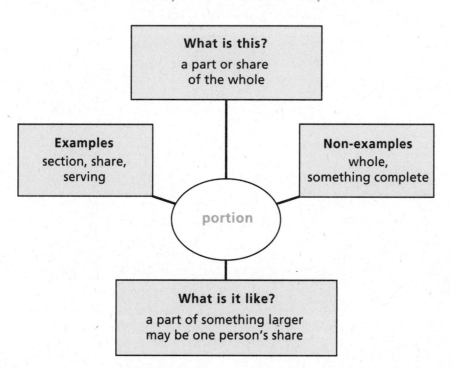

If you can fill in all the parts of this graphic organizer, you are well on your way to really knowing the word *portion*.

*Dale, E., & O'Rourke, J. (1986). *Vocabulary Building*. Columbus, OH: Zaner-Bloser.

Study the definitions of the words. Then do the exercises that follow.

abate
ə bāt´

v. To become weaker; to decrease.
The speaker waited until the applause had **abated** before continuing.

unabated *adj.* Showing no sign of weakening; showing no decrease.
Representative Millet showed **unabated** enthusiasm for campaigning for the senate seat, even though he had been twice defeated for that office.

. . . .

Show your partner how you look when your energy abates.

acknowledge
ak näl´ ij

v. 1. To admit the existence of.
Did the teacher **acknowledge** that you had turned in your paper?

2. To express recognition or thanks for.
The new Wimbledon singles champion raised her hand to **acknowledge** the cheers of the crowd.

acknowledged *adj.* Commonly accepted or recognized.
Bill James is an **acknowledged** expert on baseball.

. . . .

Chat with your partner about what you do or say to acknowledge a friend who walks past you.

agent
ā´ jənt

n. 1. A person who acts or does business for another.
The author's **agent** found a company to publish his latest mystery story.

2. Something that brings about a result.
A new principal can be a powerful **agent** for change in a school.

authority
ə thôr´ ə tē

n. 1. The right to give orders, make decisions, or take action.
Only the Congress of the United States has the **authority** to declare war.

2. An expert source of information.
The researcher Jane Goodall is a world **authority** on chimpanzees.

authorities *n.* A group of people who have the right to enforce laws.
The **authorities** closed the restaurant because it did not meet the proper standards for cleanliness.

. . . .

Tell your partner about a hobby or topic you are an authority on.

devastate
dev´ ə stāt

v. To ruin or destroy completely.
Farmers in the Midwest fear that lack of rain will **devastate** the wheat crop.

devastating *adj.* Causing destruction.
A **devastating** hurricane destroyed hundreds of homes in southern Florida.

devastation *n.* Great destruction.
The earthquake in Japan created a scene of massive **devastation.**

. . . .

Discuss with your partner how rain, wind, or snow can cause devastation.

epidemic
ep ə dem´ ik

n. The rapid spreading of a disease to many people at one time.
The flu **epidemic** of 1918 killed over twenty million people in the Northern Hemisphere.

adj. Spreading rapidly as a disease over a wide area.
AIDS became **epidemic** in central Africa in the 1980s.

estimate
es´ tə mət

n. A number that is not exact; a careful guess.
The mechanic's **estimate** for repairing the car is $1000.

v. (es´ tə māt) To figure out roughly; to make an approximate calculation.
We **estimate** that it will take the bus driver an hour to drive us to the museum.

. . . .

Work with your partner to quickly estimate how many chairs there are in your classroom.

evict
ē vikt´

v. To force out of property by taking legal action.
The landlord threatened to **evict** the tenants for not paying the rent.

impartial
im pär´ shəl

adj. Not favoring one side more than another; fair.
A judge should be **impartial** in the courtroom.

industrious
in dus´ trē əs

adj. Hardworking; not lazy.
The more **industrious** students were rewarded at the end of the year with scholarships.

infuriate
in fyoor´ ē āt

v. To make very angry.
Cruelty to animals **infuriates** me.

. . . .

Share with your partner something that infuriates you.

irrelevant
ir rel´ ə vənt

adj. Having nothing to do with the subject.
It's **irrelevant** whether I want to go to the party because I'm too sick to go.

precise
pri sīs´

adj. Exact; specific.
Do you know the **precise** time that your class starts?

precision *n.* (pri sizh´ ən) Exactness.
An eye surgeon's work requires great **precision.**

Tell your partner the precise number of purple things you can see right now.

sham
sham

n. Something fake or false.
Their offer to make us rich turned out to be a **sham.**

adj. Not genuine; fake.
Although he tried to appear sorry, his **sham** apology fooled no one.

v. To pretend.
We **shammed** illness so we could stay home.

trek
trek

n. A long, slow, and difficult journey.
The hikers were exhausted after their **trek** over the mountain.

v. To travel slowly and with difficulty.
Sam **trekked** ten miles into town after his car broke down.

1A Finding Meanings

Choose two phrases to form a sentence that correctly uses a word from Word List 1. Then write the sentence.

1. (a) you make that person very angry. (c) If you infuriate someone,
   (b) you act in that person's place.   (d) If you evict someone,

_____

_____

2. (a) something that is not genuine. (c) An estimate is
   (b) a decrease in size or amount.   (d) A sham is

_____

_____

3. (a) a disease that spreads rapidly. (c) An epidemic is
   (b) a number that is not exact.   (d) An agent is

_____

_____

4. (a) that is meant to be helpful.   (c) A devastating comment is one
   (b) An irrelevant comment is one   (d) that is off the subject.

   _____

   _____

5. (a) An agent is   (c) something that cannot be explained.
   (b) A trek is   (d) something that produces a result.

   _____

   _____

6. (a) one who works hard.   (c) An industrious person is
   (b) An impartial person is   (d) one who is highly paid.

   _____

   _____

7. (a) Estimates are   (c) people who enforce the law.
   (b) Authorities are   (d) witnesses to an accident.

   _____

   _____

8. (a) is strongly denied.   (c) Something that is acknowledged
   (b) is generally accepted.   (d) Something that is unabated

   _____

   _____

9. (a) a state of destruction.   (c) Precision is
   (b) Devastation is   (d) a sticking or holding together.

   _____

   _____

10. (a) An authority is   (c) an expert source of information.
    (b) a decrease in force or power.   (d) A trek is

   _____

   _____

| abate |
| acknowledge |
| agent |
| authority |
| devastate |
| epidemic |
| estimate |
| evict |
| impartial |
| industrious |
| infuriate |
| irrelevant |
| precise |
| sham |
| trek |

Replace each phrase in bold with a single word (or form of the word) from the word list.

1. The people had no right to be there, so they were **removed by force** from the house.

2. The teacher has the **right to give orders** to send students to the principal's office.

3. Those judging the contest are expected to be **fair and not to favor either side.**

4. The parts of a jigsaw puzzle must be cut with **very great care** if they are to fit together properly.

5. In a special ceremony, the town **expressed its gratitude for** the firefighters.

6. To succeed in the movie business, you need a good **person to represent you.**

7. Natalia will **give a rough idea of** how many pencils we need.

8. We waited for the traffic to **decrease in volume** before we left the city.

9. Yesterday's tornado in eastern Kansas **completely ruined** a neighborhood.

10. We **made a long and difficult journey** across the desert for three days.

Circle the letter or letters next to each correct answer. There may be more than one correct answer.

1. Which of the following can be **shammed?**
   - (a) concern
   - (b) honesty
   - (c) sleep
   - (d) interest

2. Which of the following might be **estimated?**
   - (a) the cost of repairs
   - (b) the height of a hill
   - (c) the population of a town
   - (d) the number of days in a week

3. Which of the following would be **irrelevant** in judging a student's writing?
   - (a) the student's age
   - (b) the student's name
   - (c) the width of the margins
   - (d) the color of the ink used

4. Which of the following might result in someone's being **evicted** from a house?
   - (a) failing to pay the rent
   - (b) using it for illegal purposes
   - (c) causing damage to it
   - (d) taking good care of it

5. Which of the following can **abate?**
   - (a) anger
   - (b) high winds
   - (c) silence
   - (d) applause

6. Which of the following are **precise** amounts?
   - (a) 2,145
   - (b) several hundred
   - (c) half a dozen
   - (d) a lot

7. Which of the following might be considered a **trek?**
   - (a) a trip to the corner store
   - (b) a ride in a hot-air balloon
   - (c) a walk across Canada
   - (d) a plane trip to Europe

8. Which of the following would be **devastating** to a town?
   - (a) a new mayor
   - (b) an earthquake
   - (c) a shopping mall
   - (d) a celebration

abate
acknowledge
agent
authority
devastate
epidemic
estimate
evict
impartial
industrious
infuriate
irrelevant
precise
sham
trek

1D Word Study: Synonyms and Antonyms

Circle the two synonyms in each group of four words.

1. authority	expert	agent	practice
2. admit	acknowledge	forget	devastate
3. calculation	decision	estimate	trek
4. secret	irrelevant	fair	impartial
5. weak	fake	precise	sham
6. increase	destroy	devastate	infuriate

Circle the two antonyms in each group of words.

7. abate	rule	increase	evict
8. trek	deny	infuriate	soothe
9. epidemic	precise	inaccurate	angry
10. industrious	irrelevant	strong	lazy

1E Vocabulary in Context

Read the passage.

The Trail of Tears

The original inhabitants of what is now Kentucky and Tennessee were an **industrious** people who lived mainly by hunting and farming. They were called Cherokees by the Europeans who first made contact with them. The Europeans had settled along the East Coast in the early 1600s. These first meetings between European traders and Cherokees were friendly but were to have **devastating** consequences for the Native Americans later. The Europeans brought goods for trading, it's true. But they also brought smallpox, a disease that had been unknown in North America before their arrival. This disease left the body covered with sores and was often fatal. In 1745, a smallpox **epidemic** struck the Cherokee people. It killed more than half the population. And that was just the beginning of the Cherokee people's woes.

The United States government recognized the Cherokee Nation as a separate country and **acknowledged** its right to sign treaties, or legally binding agreements, with other countries. In treaty after treaty, the Cherokees gave more and more of their land to the United States government. In return, they gained the right to **evict** anyone who settled illegally on the remaining land. But settlers ignored these agreements. They continued to move onto Cherokee land in great numbers. The United States government did not even pretend to be **impartial** in the disputes that arose as a result. The appeals of the Cherokee leaders fell on deaf ears. The theft of their land continued **unabated.** By 1828, the Cherokee Nation was one-tenth the size it had been a hundred years earlier.

In 1835, an **agent** of the United States government persuaded twenty Cherokees to sign one final treaty. According to its terms, the Cherokees would get five million dollars for leaving the last of their land and moving almost a thousand miles west. The Cherokee signers had no **authority** to act for the entire Cherokee Nation, but this fact was brushed aside as **irrelevant** by those in the government who wanted the land. The chief justice of the United States declared the agreement a **sham.** His opinion **infuriated** President Andrew Jackson, who replied, "The chief justice has made his decision; now let him enforce it."

Precisely two years after the signing of the agreement, on the orders of the president, two thousand heavily armed United States soldiers arrived on Cherokee land. They drove the Cherokee families from their homes. Nearly twenty thousand people were forced to **trek** more than nine hundred miles west into what is now Oklahoma. They went mostly on foot. It has been **estimated** that about four thousand Native Americans died on the journey, which became known as the "Trail of Tears." In a sense, though, the Cherokees had traveled an even longer and even more sorrowful trail, a journey in time that began when the unsuspecting Cherokees first greeted the Europeans as friends.

▶ **Answer each of the following questions with a sentence. If a question does not contain a vocabulary word from the lesson's word list, use one in your answer. Use each word only once.**

1. Why did smallpox kill so many Cherokees in such a short time?

_____

_____

| abate |
| acknowledge |
| agent |
| authority |
| devastate |
| epidemic |
| estimate |
| evict |
| impartial |
| industrious |
| infuriate |
| irrelevant |
| precise |
| sham |
| trek |

2. About how many Cherokees died of smallpox in 1745?

_____

_____

3. Did the Cherokees' repeated appeals to the United States government slow down the theft of their land?

_____

_____

4. What is the meaning of **agent** as it is used in the passage?

_____

_____

5. Why was the Cherokees' last treaty a **sham?**

_____

_____

6. Why might we think that the Cherokees were successful farmers?

_____

_____

7. Were those who wanted the Cherokees' land influenced by the fact that the Cherokee signers of the 1835 treaty had acted illegally?

_____

_____

8. What is the meaning of **acknowledged** as it is used in the passage?

_____

_____

9. Why do you think President Jackson was **infuriated** by the chief justice's opinion?

_____

_____

10. What is the meaning of **authority** as it is used in the passage?

_____

_____

11. What happened when the Cherokees tried to **evict** illegal settlers?

_____

_____

12. How should the United States government have behaved in dealing with the disputes between the Cherokees and the white settlers?

_____

_____

13. How far did the Cherokees have to travel to get to what is now Oklahoma?

_____

_____

14. Is the figure of twenty thousand persons forced out of their homes an exact one?

_____

_____

15. What kind of effect did the forced removal of the Cherokees from their land have on them?

_____

_____

abate
acknowledge
agent
authority
devastate
epidemic
estimate
evict
impartial
industrious
infuriate
irrelevant
precise
sham
trek

Fun & Fascinating FACTS

- An **epidemic** disease spreads rapidly and affects many people. (Polio was *epidemic* in the U.S. in the 1950s.) An *endemic* disease occurs normally in an area because of the conditions in that area. (Malaria is *endemic* to tropical Africa.)

- **Trek** comes from an old Dutch word *treck,* meaning "to pull or drag." Dutch settlers in South Africa used the word when describing their journeys by covered wagon because they often had to drag the wagons themselves. The English word, therefore, has come to mean any long, slow, difficult journey.

- *Industry* is a noun and means (1) "a branch of business or manufacturing" (the automobile *industry;* the film *industry*), and (2) "a willingness to work hard" (The teacher praised the student's *industry*). The two adjectives formed from this noun relate to its two different meanings. *Industrial* means "having to do with business or manufacturing." (The United States and Japan are two of the world's leading *industrial* nations.) **Industrious** relates to the second meaning of *industry.*

Vocabulary Extension

estimate

verb To figure out roughly; to make an approximate calculation.

noun A number that is not exact; a careful guess.

Academic Context

You may often be asked to **estimate** things when precise numbers are not quick or easy to figure out.

Sometimes you might **estimate** before counting or measuring something, and then you might compare your **estimate** to the exact number or measurement.

Discussion & Writing Prompt

Describe the last time you **estimated** something. How did you make a careful guess?

2 min.	3 min.
1. Turn and talk to your partner or group.	2. Write 2–4 sentences.
Use this space to take notes or draw your ideas.	Be ready to share what you have written.

Study the definitions of the words. Then do the exercises that follow.

astute ə sto͞ot´	*adj.* Wise in a clever or practical way. An **astute** shopper compares prices carefully before making a purchase.

authentic
ô then´ tik

adj. Genuine; true.
An authority on old maps declared that the sixteenth-century chart of the Florida Keys is **authentic**.

authenticity *n.* (ô then tis´ i tē) The condition of being genuine.
Lawyers questioned the **authenticity** of the signature on the agreement.

authenticate *v.* To prove that something is genuine.
Only an art expert can **authenticate** the painting as one by Rubens.

Describe for your partner a time when you found out something was fake and not authentic.

delicacy
del´ i kə sē

n. 1. A choice item of food.
Smoked salmon is a **delicacy**.

2. Great consideration for the feelings of others.
Discussing her mistake will embarrass her unless you handle the matter with **delicacy**.

Discuss with your partner a situation you would need to handle with delicacy.

derogatory
də räg´ ə tôr ē

adj. Expressing a low opinion; intended to hurt the reputation of a person or thing.
His habit of making **derogatory** comments about other students made him unpopular.

Tell your partner a derogatory comment you heard about a famous person, and explain why it was rude.

devour
də vour´

v. 1. To eat up hungrily.
We were so hungry after school, we **devoured** all the fruit in the refrigerator.

2. To take in eagerly with the eyes or ears.
We **devoured** the graphic novels the librarian gave us.

Describe to your partner the last thing you devoured.

figment
fig´ mənt

n. Something that is made up in the mind but that has no connection with reality.
The monster in the closet is a **figment** of the child's imagination.

mythical mith´i kəl	*adj.* Imaginary; not real. Unicorns are **mythical** creatures.

plumage plo͞om´ ij	*n.* A bird's feathers. Parrots have brightly colored **plumage.**

predatory pred´ ə tôr ē	*adj.* 1. Living by killing and eating other animals. Crocodiles are **predatory** reptiles. 2. Living by using, controlling, or hurting others. **Predatory** bands of pirates once sailed the Mediterranean seeking victims. **predator** *n.* 1. A creature that lives by killing. A sea eagle is a **predator** that dives for fish. 2. A person who looks for others to use, control, or hurt them in some way. The Vikings were **predators** who terrified coastal towns.

prior prī´ ər	*adj.* 1. Coming earlier in time. I was unable to see you this morning because I had a **prior** appointment. 2. Coming before in order or importance. The court ruled that the Native Americans had a **prior** claim to the land. *Share with your partner something that happened to you just prior to coming to school.*

scavenge skav´ ənj	*v.* To search through or pick over, looking for something usable. People with metal detectors **scavenge** the beach looking for coins. **scavenger** *n.* 1. Someone who scavenges. After the fire, **scavengers** looked through the debris, hoping to find something of value. 2. An animal that feeds on dead or decaying matter. Vultures, hyenas, and other **scavengers** are an important part of nature's clean-up crew.

slaughter slôt´ ər	*v.* 1. To kill in order to obtain meat. The hogs are rounded up before they are **slaughtered.** 2. To kill people or animals in large numbers or in a cruel way. For centuries, whales have been **slaughtered** for their oil and other valuable products. *n.* 1. The killing of an animal for food. The **slaughter** of beef cattle should be carried out as swiftly and painlessly as possible. 2. The act of killing on a large scale or in a cruel way. Those who drink and drive contribute to the **slaughter** on the nation's highways.

solitude säl´ ə tōod	*n.* The condition of being alone or at some distance from people. We enjoyed the **solitude** of a walk on the deserted beach. *Talk to your partner about a moment of solitude that you had recently.*
ungainly un gān´ lē	*adj.* Moving in a clumsy or awkward way. Walruses, graceful in the water, are **ungainly** creatures on land.
vulnerable vul´ nər ə bəl	*adj.* Open to attack; easily injured physically or emotionally. Elderly people are more **vulnerable** to disease than younger people. *Discuss how someone acts when he or she is feeling vulnerable.*

2A Using Words in Context

Read the following sentences. If the word in bold is used correctly, write C on the line. If the word is used incorrectly, write I on the line.

1. (a) I **slaughtered** dozens of ants with bug spray. ___
   (b) Mass **slaughter** of the American bison almost led to its extinction. ___
   (c) You put your mail in a **slaughter.** ___
   (d) Gales of **slaughter** greeted the speaker's jeers. ___

astute
authentic
delicacy
derogatory
devour
figment
mythical
plumage
predatory
prior
scavenge
slaughter
solitude
ungainly
vulnerable

2. (a) We had a **prior** agreement with the neighbors that we could buy the puppy. ___
   (b) Sixth grade takes place **prior** to seventh grade. ___
   (c) **Prior** to the storm, the wind buffeted the trees back and forth. ___
   (d) First, hold your cup, and then pour some **prior** water into it. ___

3. (a) The Egyptian coin I found in my backyard can't be **authentic.** ___
   (b) The **authenticity** of the rare book was confirmed by scholars. ___
   (c) These dinosaur bones have not been **authenticated** by experts. ___
   (d) The Robinsons felt exhausted and **authentic** after the long day. ___

4. (a) When the water in the fish tank gets **derogatory,** it's time to clean it. ___
   (b) I didn't mean to sound **derogatory,** and I'm sorry if I hurt your feelings. ___
   (c) I heard several **derogatory** comments on the television show. ___
   (d) The runner jogged through the warm **derogatory** sunshine. ___

5. (a) I wasn't hungry at all, so I **devoured** the food. ___
   (b) By the time it was put out, the fire had **devoured** over a thousand acres. ___
   (c) Alyssa **devoured** novels by the dozen. ___
   (d) The hikers **devoured** the food hungrily and then rested. ___

6. (a) Snails are a **delicacy** to many people. ___
   (b) The matter was handled with great **delicacy,** and no one's feelings were hurt. ___
   (c) A tall **delicacy** grew outside the kitchen door. ___
   (d) We checked all the **delicacies** on the bike before I rode it. ___

7. (a) His **ungainly** gait was explained by a childhood accident. ___
   (b) The **ungainly** professional ballerina twirled gracefully across the stage. ___
   (c) Penguins look **ungainly** until they flop into the water. ___
   (d) Jayden's **ungainly** water was cold and refreshing. ___

8. (a) Hakim **astutely** observed that without extra funding, the library would shut down. ___
   (b) The silly, **astute** dog tripped over the hose and fell on its face. ___
   (c) Gabriella believed she was **astute** enough to fool her parents. ___
   (d) The ice was **astute** enough to easily support our weight. ___

9. (a) Try to **scavenge** whatever you can from the beach. ___
   (b) **Scavengers** are at the bottom of the food chain, living on leftovers. ___
   (c) A good soccer player can **scavenge** a few goals every game. ___
   (d) The baby would fall over every time it tried to **scavenge.** ___

10. (a) Jules attended a **predatory** school before going to college. ___
    (b) A **predatory** rainstorm misted the meadow with dew. ___
    (c) **Predatory** thieves roamed the land outside the castle. ___
    (d) In the animal kingdom, you can be both **predator** and prey. ___

Making Connections

Circle the letter next to each correct answer. There may be more than one correct answer.

1. Which word or words go with *not real?*
   (a) authentic   (b) figment   (c) fanciful   (d) mythical

2. Which word or words go with *bird?*
   (a) mythical   (b) plumage   (c) ungainly   (d) authentic

3. Which word or words go with *alone?*
   (a) solitary   (b) solar   (c) solid   (d) solitude

4. Which word or words go with *weak?*
   (a) feeble   (b) derogatory   (c) puny   (d) vulnerable

5. Which word or words go with *smart?*
   (a) authentic   (b) brilliant   (c) ungainly   (d) astute

6. Which word or words go with *eat?*
   (a) authentic   (b) consume   (c) devour   (d) plumage

7. Which word or words go with *real?*
   (a) authentic   (b) genuine   (c) mythical   (d) casual

8. Which word or words go with *insult?*
   (a) devour   (b) derogatory   (c) compete   (d) slaughter

9. Which word or words go with *kill?*
   (a) scavenge   (b) exterminate   (c) slay   (d) slaughter

10. Which word or words go with *awkward?*
    (a) unwieldy   (b) ungainly   (c) unruly   (d) vulnerable

astute
authentic
delicacy
derogatory
devour
figment
mythical
plumage
predatory
prior
scavenge
slaughter
solitude
ungainly
vulnerable

2C

Determining Meanings

Circle the letter next to each answer choice that correctly completes the sentence. There may be more than one correct answer.

1. **Figments**
   (a) of the imagination might be a unicorn, dragon, and mermaid.
   (b) grow on trees where the climate is warm.
   (c) of stone flew into the windshield and cracked it.
   (d) of a child's mind, like monsters, can be scary.

2. A **prior**
   (a) cake was brought in, and Luisa blew out the candles.
   (b) meeting established the rules that were to be followed.
   (c) expedition had failed to reach the South Pole.
   (d) problem was solved, but a new problem took its place.

3. **Scavengers**
   (a) in the sky shone down on the forest.
   (b) like vultures are a necessary part of nature.
   (c) might spend a lot of time going through trash cans and dumpsters.
   (d) of poetry might enjoy this first edition.

4. The **mythical**
   (a) hero inspired many stories.
   (b) land called Atlantis may have once existed.
   (c) deep breath made me feel more calm.
   (d) answer could mean yes or no.

5. The **plumage**
   (a) of eagles was used by North American tribes.
   (b) of penguins protects them against the severe cold.
   (c) of egrets was used to decorate ladies' hats.
   (d) of a snake is shed several times during its life.

6. **Solitude**
   (a) was welcome after the hectic day at school.
   (b) provided inspiration for the poet's early writing about loneliness.
   (c) on the edges of the window looked like lace.
   (d) was impossible for someone leading such a busy life.

7. **Vulnerability**
   (a) around the pond turned to sticky mud.
   (b) can make a person easily hurt.
   (c) can turn black to gray.
   (d) is a characteristic of newborn babies.

8. An **astutely**
   (a) blue paint decorated the walls.
   (b) wise person would have guessed the answer right away.
   (c) sad face could be seen in the window.
   (d) intelligent book about school safety was published last week.

2D Completing Sentences

Complete the sentences to demonstrate your knowledge of the words in bold.

1. Something that is a **figment** of the imagination is

   _____ .

2. I am most **vulnerable** when

   _____ .

3. If an old letter is **authentic,** that means

   _____ .

4. My favorite **mythical** creature is

   _____ .

5. An animal that **scavenges** looks for

   _____ .

6. A **derogatory** remark would make me feel

   _____ .

7. When I want **solitude,** I

   _____ .

8. You may want to handle a situation with **delicacy** because

   _____ .

9. An **ungainly** person would find it hard to

   _____ .

10. To **devour** something, you have to be

   _____ .

astute
authentic
delicacy
derogatory
devour
figment
mythical
plumage
predatory
prior
scavenge
slaughter
solitude
ungainly
vulnerable

The Last Dodo

If someone referred to you as a "dodo," you would probably be insulted. It is a **derogatory** term that describes someone who is not very **astute.** The origin of the English word can be traced back to the Portuguese *duodo,* which means "a foolish person." Dodo was the name Portuguese settlers gave to the large, flightless bird that inhabited the island of Mauritius in the Indian Ocean. Some people think of the dodo as a **mythical** creature. It is a fact that this was a real bird, however, and its story is a sad one.

For thousands of years, until the island of Mauritius was discovered by Portuguese sailors in 1507, this odd-looking bird existed in peaceful **solitude.** Because there were no **predatory** animals on the island, the dodo had long since lost the ability to fly. And, because it lacked natural enemies, it was very trusting and made no attempt to flee when approached by humans. Because of this, the Portuguese considered the bird stupid and gave it the name by which we know it today—the dodo.

Even if it had been less trusting of humans, the dodo would still have been **vulnerable.** It was too overweight and **ungainly** to run very fast. The settlers on the island found that dodos, although a little tough, were good to eat, and they **slaughtered** them in ever-increasing numbers. Domesticated animals brought to the island by the settlers added to the dodos' problems. The female dodo laid a single large white egg, which it deposited on the ground, usually in a tuft of grass. **Prior** to the arrival of the original settlers, the eggs had lain undisturbed until they hatched. To the dogs that now roamed the island, these eggs were a **delicacy;** the dogs **scavenged** the island and **devoured** any dodo eggs they encountered. The dodo was last seen alive in 1681. None is believed to have survived after that date.

As time passed, people began to wonder if the dodo had ever existed. Drawings done by artists who had visited Mauritius showed a bird somewhat larger than a swan, with an elongated neck, a large head, an enormous black bill, and a short, tufty tail. Its **plumage** was grayish in color over most of its body and white on its breast. The majority of people who saw these pictures convinced themselves that such an odd-looking creature must be a **figment** of the artist's imagination; at that time, there was no way of establishing whether they provided an **authentic** record of an actual creature.

Then, in 1889, a large number of dodo bones were discovered in a swamp on Mauritius. Several skeletons were reconstructed from them and subsequently displayed in museums in London and Paris. These relics are all that remain of this odd-looking but rather lovable bird.

▶ **Answer each of the following questions with a sentence. If a question does not contain a vocabulary word from the lesson's word list, use one in your answer. Use each word only once.**

1. What drastic change occurred in the dodos' living conditions in 1507?

_____

_____

2. What is the meaning of **prior** as it is used in the passage?

_____

_____

3. What was it about the dodo's nature that made it easy to catch?

_____

_____

4. What was it about the dodo's physical condition that made it easy to catch?

_____

_____

5. What other names of birds are **derogatory** when applied to humans?

_____

_____

6. How was the existence of the dodo **authenticated?**

_____

_____

7. What did the Portuguese think of the dodo's intelligence?

_____

_____

8. What is the meaning of **delicacy** as it is used in the passage?

_____

_____

| astute |
| authentic |
| delicacy |
| derogatory |
| devour |
| figment |
| mythical |
| plumage |
| predatory |
| prior |
| scavenge |
| slaughter |
| solitude |
| ungainly |
| vulnerable |

9. What color were a dodo's feathers?

_____

_____

10. What is the meaning of **devoured** as it is used in the passage?

_____

_____

11. Why did many people believe the dodo to be a **figment** of an artist's imagination?

_____

_____

12. What did people think about the dodo before the discovery of the bones?

_____

_____

13. What is the meaning of **slaughtered** as it is used in the passage?

_____

_____

14. What is the meaning of **predatory** as it is used in the passage?

_____

_____

15. How would you describe the dogs that lived on the island?

_____

Fun & Fascinating FACTS

- The Latin for *feather* is *pluma*. In addition to the word **plumage,** this Latin root gives us the English word *plume,* which is a noun, meaning "a large feather or group of feathers," and a verb, meaning "to smooth its feathers." (Birds *plume* themselves with their beaks.) The French word for *pen* is *plume* and comes from the same Latin root. Pens were once made from large feathers with the ends split to hold ink.

- The Latin *solus* means "alone" or "without company" and forms the root of a number of English words in addition to **solitude.** *Solitaire* is a card game for just one person. *Solitary* means "alone" or "without company." *Solo* means "performed by one person."

2 **V**ocabulary **E**xtension

authentic

adjective Real; true.

Synonyms and Antonyms
Synonyms: genuine, original, actual
Antonyms: inauthentic, fake, untrue

Discussion & Writing Prompt

Describe something that is not **authentic.**

2 min.	3 min.
1. Turn and talk to your partner or group.	2. Write 2–4 sentences.
Use this space to take notes or draw your ideas.	Be ready to share what you have written.

Study the definitions of the words. Then do the exercises that follow.

admonish
ad män´ ish

v. 1. To warn.
Rescue workers **admonished** us to stay away from the flooding river.

2. To criticize gently.
The coach **admonished** me for missing practice.

admonition *n.* (ad mə nish´ ən) A warning.
We remembered our parents' **admonition** to stay close to shore while swimming.

Tell your partner one admonition you have heard a teacher give.

aghast
ə gast´

adj. Struck with horror; shocked.
We were **aghast** at what the storm had done to the neighborhood.

annihilate
ə nī´ ə lāt

v. To destroy completely; to reduce to utter ruin.
General Custer's army of over two hundred men was **annihilated** at the battle of the Little Bighorn in 1876.

benefactor
ben´ ə fak tər

n. A person who provides help, especially by giving money.
People who donated more than $100 were listed as **benefactors** of the library.

bestow
bē stō´

v. To give as an honor; to present as a gift.
An Academy Award is the highest honor Hollywood can **bestow** on a film.

Bestow your pencil upon your partner.

devious
dē´ vē əs

adj. 1. Having many twists and turns; winding.
The climbers followed a **devious** route up the mountain.

2. Sneaky; not frank or honest.
This **devious** scheme was intended to take advantage of vulnerable people.

Chat with your partner about something a devious person might do.

devoid
də void´

adj. Lacking; empty; entirely without.
Although he had experienced great misfortune, he was **devoid** of bitterness.

Discuss with your partner how you might feel if you were devoid of happiness.

heed hēd	*v.* To pay attention to. I hope you will **heed** my advice. *n.* Attention; notice. Pay **heed** to the teacher's instructions before you begin the test. **heedful** *adj.* Paying careful attention. **Heedful** of the fog, my uncle drove slowly. **heedless** *adj.* Failing to pay proper attention. They went ahead with their plans, **heedless** of our objections.
mortal môrt´l	*n.* A human being, especially as contrasted with a god. Achilles, a hero in Greek mythology, had a goddess for a mother and a **mortal** for a father. *adj.* 1. Of or relating to human beings. Being **mortal,** he accepted the fact that one day he would die. 2. Causing death; fatal. Caesar received a **mortal** wound delivered by his friend Brutus. 3. Very severe. My friend wouldn't go into the reptile house because he has a **mortal** fear of snakes.
muse myōōz	*v.* To think about in a quiet, careful way. Mother **mused** over whether to sell the house.
pioneer pī ə nir´	*n.* A person who goes before others and opens the way for them to follow. Lucretia Mott and Elizabeth Cady Stanton, two nineteenth-century women, were **pioneers** in the women's rights movement. *v.* To open the way for others. Langston Hughes **pioneered** jazz poetry. .... *Talk to your partner about what it might have been like to pioneer space travel.*
plague plāg	*n.* 1. A deadly disease that spreads rapidly from person to person. Those Londoners who could afford it fled to the country to escape the great **plague** of 1665. 2. Anything that causes destruction or suffering. A **plague** of locusts destroyed the crop. *v.* To cause suffering or distress. After the tryouts, I was **plagued** by doubts that I would make the varsity team.

subside
səb sīd´

v. 1. To sink to a lower level.
After the rain stopped, the floodwaters gradually **subsided.**

2. To become quieter or less active.
The baby's sobs gradually **subsided.**

Tell your partner one thing a teacher can do to make classroom noise subside.

unwitting
un wit´ iŋ

adj. Not done on purpose; unintended.
I tried to ignore the **unwitting** insult, but his comment hurt me just the same.

wrath
rath

n. Forceful anger; fury.
When I saw the girl being bullied, I was filled with **wrath.**

wrathful *adj.* Very angry.
In Homer's story of the Trojan War, a **wrathful** Achilles seeks revenge on the killer of his friend Patroclus.

Discuss with your partner some positive steps to take when you feel wrathful.

3A Finding Meanings

Choose two phrases to form a sentence that correctly uses a word from Word List 3. Then write the sentence.

1. (a) is one that is caused deliberately.   (c) is one that causes death.
   (b) A mortal wound   (d) An unwitting injury

   _____

   _____

2. (a) helps with gifts of money.   (c) stands in the way of change.
   (b) A pioneer is someone who   (d) A benefactor is someone who

   _____

   _____

3. (a) one that is unintended.   (c) one given as a warning.
   (b) A wrathful insult is   (d) An unwitting insult is

   _____

   _____

4. (a) gradually rises.
   (b) twists and turns.

   (c) A subsiding path is one that
   (d) A devious path is one that

   _____

5. (a) fooled by false promises.
   (b) shocked.

   (c) To be aghast is to be
   (d) To be annihilated is to be

   _____

6. (a) To subside is to
   (b) do worse than expected.

   (c) To muse is to
   (d) sink to a lower level.

   _____

7. (a) To be wrathful is to
   (b) To be mortal is to

   (c) live forever.
   (d) be very angry.

   _____

8. (a) open the way for others.
   (b) express disagreement.

   (c) To muse is to
   (d) To pioneer is to

   _____

9. (a) To admonish someone is to
   (b) protect that person.

   (c) To plague someone is to
   (d) criticize that person.

   _____

10. (a) is to fail to pay attention to it.
    (b) is to be well supplied with it.

    (c) To be heedless of something
    (d) To be devoid of something

    _____

| admonish |
| aghast |
| annihilate |
| benefactor |
| bestow |
| devious |
| devoid |
| heed |
| mortal |
| muse |
| pioneer |
| plague |
| subside |
| unwitting |
| wrath |

Replace each phrase in bold with a single word (or form of the word) from the word list.

1. "What fools these **human beings** be," says Shakespeare's Puck.

2. Drug-related violence is a **cause of much suffering** that began to spread rapidly in the 1970s.

3. New Orleans was almost **reduced to ruins** in 2005 by Hurricane Katrina.

4. Elizabeth Blackwell was a **person who opened the way for others** in the field of medical education for women.

5. Drivers should **pay close attention to** stop signs.

6. Avoid doing business with Ed; he is **not honest in his dealings with others.**

7. As far as we know, Mars is **totally lacking in any form** of life.

8. In ancient times, people believed that a volcano's eruption was caused by the **terrible anger** of the gods.

9. Two children are easier to care for than one, the babysitter **thought quietly to himself.**

10. We obeyed the park ranger's **instruction that warned us** to be careful with matches while in the woods.

Circle the letter or letters next to each correct answer. There may be more than one correct answer.

1. Which of the following can **subside?**
   (a) an epidemic
   (b) the floor
   (c) a storm
   (d) flame

2. Which of the following might a **wrathful** person do?
   (a) seek revenge
   (b) apologize
   (c) make derogatory remarks
   (d) speak in a loud voice

3. Which of the following can you **heed?**
   (a) advice
   (b) a suggestion
   (c) a warning
   (d) a gift

4. Which of the following might **plague** a person?
   (a) hopes
   (b) doubts
   (c) worries
   (d) fears

5. Which of the following might make you **aghast?**
   (a) seeing a beautiful sunset
   (b) hearing of a terrible accident
   (c) missing a favorite TV show
   (d) receiving good news

6. Which of the following can be **mortal?**
   (a) terror
   (b) wounds
   (c) buildings
   (d) horses

7. Which of the following could be described as **devious?**
   (a) a winding path
   (b) an impartial judge
   (c) a person who lies and cheats
   (d) a person who lacks authority

8. Which of the following might a **benefactor** do?
   (a) pay your college tuition
   (b) support a local theater
   (c) make derogatory remarks about you
   (d) give you good advice

admonish
aghast
annihilate
benefactor
bestow
devious
devoid
heed
mortal
muse
pioneer
plague
subside
unwitting
wrath

Word Study: Latin Roots

Read the Latin words and their meanings. Then complete the sentences. The vocabulary words are from Lesson 3 or earlier.

Many English words come from Latin. We say they have Latin roots.

facere (to make)   *furor* (rage)   *monere* (to warn)   *mors* (death)
nihil (nothing)   *sidere* (to settle) *solus* (alone)   *pars* (side)
via (way)   *vulnus* (a wound)

1. To _____ someone is to warn that person. The word comes from the Latin _____ , meaning _____ .

2. _____ is the state of being alone. The word comes from the Latin _____ , meaning _____ .

3. To be _____ is to be easily hurt. The word comes from the Latin _____ , meaning _____ .

4. To _____ something is to destroy it completely. The word comes from the Latin _____ , meaning _____ .

5. A(n) _____ judge will hear both sides of an argument fairly. The word comes from the Latin _____ , meaning _____ .

6. To _____ someone is to make him extremely angry. The word comes from the Latin _____ , meaning _____ .

7. A(n) _____ person is one who is not direct and straightforward. The word comes from the Latin _____ , meaning _____ .

8. To _____ is to fall to a lower level. The word comes from the Latin _____ , meaning _____ .

9. A(n) _____ wound is one that causes death. The word comes from the Latin _____ , meaning _____ .

10. A(n) _____ is a person who tries to make things better for others. The word comes from the Latin _____ , meaning _____ .

3E Vocabulary in Context
Read the passage.

Pandora's Box

Modern English contains many words and phrases with origins that go back to ancient Greece. One of these phrases is *Pandora's Box*, which has come to mean "something that produces unexpected problems or difficulties." Take, for example, the nineteenth-century French scientist Marie Curie. She was a **pioneer** in the study of uranium, and it could be said that she opened a Pandora's Box with her research. Her work led to the splitting of the uranium atom and the development of the atomic bomb. This gave the human race, for the first time in history, the power to **annihilate** itself. The expression *Pandora's Box* comes from a Greek myth that explains how evil and suffering came into existence in a world that was originally **devoid** of them.

The story starts with Prometheus, whom the ancient Greeks looked upon as a **benefactor** of the human race. They believed that he stole fire from Zeus, the king of the gods, and gave it to human beings. To get revenge, the **wrathful** Zeus punished Prometheus by chaining him to a rock where eagles came and devoured his liver. Each night it grew back, and each day it was devoured afresh. Zeus was not satisfied with this, however; he also wanted to punish the people who had received the precious gift of fire, so he came up with a **devious** plan.

Zeus ordered his son Hephaestus, the best craftsman of the gods, to create the first woman. Her name, Pandora, means "all the gifts" because each of the gods **bestowed** a special gift upon her. Aphrodite gave her beauty. Hermes gave her the ability to be crafty. Zeus gave her a box, which he **admonished** her never to open. But he also gave her the gift of curiosity. He knew that she would not **heed** his warning.

Zeus then sent Pandora to live on Earth as a **mortal.** She married and lived happily, untroubled except for one thing. She could not stop glancing at the box that Zeus had given her. That kept her **musing** about what it contained. She was often tempted to lift the lid and peep inside. Then she would remember Zeus's warning and restrain herself. However, her curiosity, far from **subsiding,** increased with every passing day.

admonish
aghast
annihilate
benefactor
bestow
devious
devoid
heed
mortal
muse
pioneer
plague
subside
unwitting
wrath

Finally, Pandora could stand it no longer. She acted swiftly, so as to give herself no time to think. She picked up the box and opened it. Immediately, all the evils that now exist in the world flew out of Pandora's Box. Greed and envy, hatred and fear, disease and despair; all appeared on Earth for the first time. They began to **plague** humankind. Pandora was **aghast** at what she had done. She quickly slammed the lid shut. Too late! She had been Zeus's **unwitting** helper as he carried out his plan of revenge and proved his power once again.

▶ **Answer each of the following questions with a sentence. If a question does not contain a vocabulary word from the lesson's word list, use one in your answer. Use each word only once.**

1. What did Prometheus **bestow** on humankind?

_____

_____

2. What is the meaning of **subsiding** as it is used in the passage?

_____

_____

3. Did Pandora know what she was doing when she helped Zeus carry out his plan?

_____

_____

4. Why would it be incorrect to call Pandora a **benefactor** of humankind?

_____

_____

5. What is the meaning of **devious** as it is used in the passage?

_____

_____

6. What warning did Zeus give Pandora when he presented her with the box?

_____

_____

7. Did Hephaestus obey Zeus's order?

_____

_____

8. How did Zeus's gift of curiosity affect Pandora?

_____

_____

9. What is the meaning of **plague** as it is used in the passage?

_____

_____

10. Did Zeus show any pity for Prometheus?

_____

_____

11. In what way did Marie Curie take a lead in the world of science?

_____

_____

12. What is the meaning of **mortal** as it is used in the passage?

_____

_____

13. According to the myth, who suffered because of Zeus's **wrath?**

_____

_____

14. Why can we say that Marie Curie opened a Pandora's Box?

_____

_____

15. How might Marie Curie have felt if she had known that her research would lead to the atomic bomb?

_____

_____

admonish
aghast
annihilate
benefactor
bestow
devious
devoid
heed
mortal
muse
pioneer
plague
subside
unwitting
wrath

Fun & Fascinating FACTS

- The word **benefactor** is formed from two Latin roots, *bene,* which means "good" or "well," and *facare,* which means "to do; to make." The Latin word *malus* means "bad" or "evil." Using your knowledge of Latin roots, can you figure out the meaning of the word *malefactor?*

- The Latin word for "death" is *mortalis;* from it comes our word **mortal.** The antonym of *mortal,* both as an adjective and a noun, is *immortal.* As an adjective, it means "living forever" (According to Greek mythology, the gods and goddesses who lived on Mount Olympus were *immortal*), and "having lasting fame" (No writer can compare to the *immortal* William Shakespeare). As a noun, *immortal* means "a mythical being who will never die" (Athena and the other *immortals* of Mount Olympus were sometimes rivals), and "a person having lasting fame" (Jane Austen is one of the *immortals* of English literature).

- **Plague** is now the general term for any widespread and deadly disease; it once referred to a specific disease called "the *Plague,*" also known as "the Black Death," which swept through Europe and parts of Asia in the fourteenth century, killing up to three quarters of the population. A red cross on a door was a sign that someone inside the house had the disease. Spread by fleas that had bitten infected rats, it attacked many parts of the body, especially the lungs, and was almost always fatal. It has reappeared at various times over recorded history; the last great outbreak of the disease was in England in 1665.

devoid

adjective Lacking; empty; entirely without.

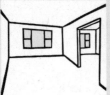

Usage Note
The word **devoid** is almost always followed by *of.*

Context Clues
These sentences give clues to the meaning of **devoid.**

> *Principal Takahashi's face was **devoid** of humor when he spoke to the class about cheating.*

> *The apartment was **devoid** of all furnishings; in fact, there wasn't even a refrigerator or stove.*

Synonyms and Antonyms
Synonyms: bare, barren, empty
Antonyms: crowded, filled, full

Discussion & Writing Prompt
Describe something you are **devoid** of right now and explain why.

2 min.	3 min.
1. Turn and talk to your partner or group.	**2.** Write 2–4 sentences.
Use this space to take notes or draw your ideas.	Be ready to share what you have written.

Study the definitions of the words. Then do the exercises that follow.

acquire
ə kwīr´

v. To gain ownership of something; to get by one's own efforts or actions.
Most tourists **acquire** souvenirs from the places they visit.

acquisition *n.* (ak wə zish´ ən) Something that is acquired.
We left the store with our shopping bags filled with our **acquisitions.**

Tell your partner about a recent acquisition you made.

antagonize
an tag´ ə nīz

v. To make an enemy of; to stir up anger or dislike.
You will **antagonize** your classmates if you make derogatory comments about them.

competent
käm´ pə tənt

adj. Having the ability to do what is needed.
The mechanic is **competent** to work on the car's brakes.

competence *n.* The ability to do what is needed.
This examination tests the student's **competence** to drive safely.

Chat with your partner about your level of competence in cooking.

comprise
kəm prīz´

v. 1. To form; to make up.
Six states **comprise** New England.

2. To consist of or include.
A baseball team **comprises** nine players.

Work with your partner to estimate how many rooms comprise your school, including classrooms, gym, cafeteria, library, and other rooms.

correspond
kôr ə spänd´

v. 1. To match; to be equal to.
The two handwriting samples **correspond** in every way.

2. To exchange letters with another person.
Although the friends hadn't seen each other for several years, they **corresponded** regularly.

correspondence *n.* The act of exchanging letters; the letters that are exchanged.
The **correspondence** of famous people is often published after their death.

dilapidated
di lap´ ə dāt əd

adj. In poor condition from neglect or age.
The shed was so **dilapidated** that it wasn't worth repairing.

illustrious il lus´ trē əs	*adj.* Very famous; outstanding. Anton Chekov, the **illustrious** Russian writer, is famous for his plays and short stories.
incident in´ sə dənt	*n.* Something that happens in real life or in a story; an event, often of little importance. Our car was struck from behind, but I thought no more about the **incident** until my neck began to hurt. *Share with your partner an amusing incident that occurred recently.*
inherit in her´ it	*v.* 1. To receive something from someone after that person's death. I **inherited** this house from my grandparents. 2. To receive, as part of one's physical or mental makeup, from one's parents. The baby **inherited** his mother's red hair.
latitude lat´ ə tōōd	*n.* 1. The distance north or south of the equator, measured in degrees. The **latitude** of New Orleans is thirty degrees north. 2. A region as marked by its distance from the equator. Tropical plants cannot survive in northern **latitudes.** 3. Freedom from strict rules. Students in high school are allowed some **latitude** in choosing their courses. *Discuss with your partner how much latitude students should have in choosing their clothes for school.*
loath lōth	*adj.* Unwilling; reluctant. I was **loath** to put my trust in such a devious person.
maintain mān tān´	*v.* 1. To declare something to be true. Although the evidence against her is strong, she continues to **maintain** her innocence. 2. To continue in the same way or condition. The walkers try to **maintain** an even pace as they exercise. 3. To keep in good condition. The state of New York **maintains** this highway. *Who do you maintain is the best athlete in history? Explain to your partner why.*
renovate ren´ ə vāt	*v.* To make like new again. My parents intend to **renovate** the apartment completely before we move in. **renovation** *n.* (ren ə vā´ shən) The act of renovating; the thing renovated. A group of concerned parents was responsible for the **renovation** of the playground.

reprimand	*v.* To scold in a harsh or formal manner.
rep´ rə mand	The principal **reprimanded** us for being late to school.
	n. A strong scolding from someone in authority.
	The teacher gave us a **reprimand** for being absent without permission.

supervise	*v.* To direct or manage activities.
sōō´ pər vīz	Ms. Agostino will **supervise** the students in the study hall.
	supervision *n.* (sōō´ pər vizh´ ən) The act of managing or directing.
	A lack of proper **supervision** resulted in yesterday's accident at the playground.
	supervisor *n.* A person who manages or directs activities.
	The **supervisor** reminded the worker to wear a hardhat at the construction site.

. . . .

Tell your partner how much supervision you think seventh graders need at a party.

4A Using Words in Context

Read the following sentences. If the word in bold is used correctly, write C on the line. If the word is used incorrectly, write I on the line.

1. (a) Ari's hobby of **corresponding** with famous people made him well known. ___
   (b) The **correspondence** of state officials is available to the public. ___
   (c) The copy should **correspond** in every way with the original. ___
   (d) One day I mean to **correspond** the story of my early life. ___

2. (a) You really need to work on your bad **latitude.** ___
   (b) The **latitude** tells us how far from the equator a place is. ___
   (c) Penguins are found only in southern **latitudes** near the pole. ___
   (d) I would like some **latitude** in where I have my birthday party. ___

3. (a) Tiana **maintains** that she and Dolores were childhood friends. ___
   (b) Nathan **maintained** an even pace until the last hundred yards of the marathon. ___
   (c) We were **maintained** in the principal's office but released almost immediately. ___
   (d) The city **maintains** all three public parks and does a fine job. ___

4. (a) I **loath** having to babysit my little brother. ___
   (b) People were **loath** to leave their homes during the epidemic. ___
   (c) When sharks were sighted offshore, the mayor was **loath** to issue a warning. ___
   (d) I was feeling **loath,** so I decided to stay home from school. ___

5. (a) Elsie likes to go to **dilapidated** lunch with her aunt every Saturday. ___
   (b) The book was in **dilapidated** condition and was practically worthless. ___
   (c) **Dilapidated** structures that cannot be repaired are demolished. ___
   (d) Alligators in Florida have increased in number in recent **dilapidated** years. ___

6. (a) Marina **acquired** a British accent shortly after arriving in London. ___
   (b) The United States **acquired** control of Texas from Mexico in 1845. ___
   (c) You are **acquired** to have your bags inspected at the gate. ___
   (d) "What's inside the box?" Alex **acquired.** ___

7. (a) The teacher promised more strict **supervision** of the book club. ___
   (b) I was shocked to **supervise** that my room had been cleaned. ___
   (c) Parents are expected to **supervise** their own children on the playground. ___
   (d) Mustafa wore a hat to **supervise** his eyes from the sun. ___

8. (a) Pour the **competence** in the jug and place it on the table. ___
   (b) A **competent** person is needed to help the teacher. ___
   (c) You can measure **competence** by studying how people respond to a crisis. ___
   (d) The racers lined up for the start of the 100-meter **competence.** ___

9. (a) The **renovation** of the United States Capitol dome took several years. ___
   (b) The computer was a **renovation** that changed life forever. ___
   (c) The sports arena was **renovated** in time for the championship game. ___
   (d) Bells **renovated** throughout the city as the people celebrated. ___

10. (a) I dropped the **incident** when it got too hot to carry. ___
    (b) The **incident** was caught on camera. ___
    (c) The **incident** happened so long ago, I had completely forgotten about it. ___
    (d) Malik remembers every little **incident** in his life. ___

acquire
antagonize
competent
comprise
correspond
dilapidated
illustrious
incident
inherit
latitude
loath
maintain
renovate
reprimand
supervise

Making Connections

Circle the letter next to each correct answer. There may be more than one correct answer.

1. Which word or words go with *obtain?*
   (a) antagonize   (b) acquire   (c) attain   (d) purchase

2. Which word or words go with *unwilling?*
   (a) loath   (b) loathe   (c) competent   (d) reluctant

3. Which word or words go with *ability?*
   (a) competent   (b) latitude   (c) capable   (d) devious

4. Which word or words go with *event?*
   (a) occasion   (b) incident   (c) reprimand   (d) latitude

5. Which word or words go with *communicate?*
   (a) inherit   (b) correspond   (c) antagonize   (d) supervise

6. Which word or words go with *scold?*
   (a) acquire   (b) reprimand   (c) supervise   (d) admonish

7. Which word or words go with *anger?*
   (a) aggravate   (b) antagonize   (c) infuriate   (d) maintain

8. Which word or words go with *include?*
   (a) admonish   (b) inherit   (c) comprise   (d) reprimand

9. Which word or words go with *famous?*
   (a) celebrated   (b) melancholy   (c) illustrious   (d) competent

10. Which word or words go with *property?*
    (a) evict   (b) inherit   (c) latitude   (d) renovate

Circle the letter next to each answer choice that correctly completes the sentence. There may be more than one correct answer.

1. We **inherited**
   (a) so much about the test last week.
   (b) the necklaces from our grandmother.
   (c) our blue eyes from our father.
   (d) the championship from the other team.

2. She **maintained**
   (a) that her favorite drink is lemonade.
   (b) a certain distance between herself and the dog.
   (c) stories about the old house on the hill.
   (d) that you can always beat your fears.

3. The **renovation**
   (a) at the edge of the plate is beautiful.
   (b) of the houses made them seem almost new.
   (c) bounced across the desert on new tires.
   (d) of the bridge kept it from collapsing.

4. Meryl **antagonizes**
   (a) people who are supposed to be her friends.
   (b) the umpire whenever he makes a call she doesn't like.
   (c) over problems every night before she goes to sleep.
   (d) to school every day, even if it rains.

5. An **illustrious**
   (a) name in American history is Chief Joseph.
   (b) hero like Harriet Tubman is a role model for us all.
   (c) lotion is on the shelf if you need it.
   (d) name from the ancient world is Cleopatra.

6. The **reprimanding**
   (a) went on all afternoon in the principal's office.
   (b) praised the student for bravery.
   (c) from the officer was a serious matter.
   (d) wind knocked over the old oak tree.

acquire
antagonize
competent
comprise
correspond
dilapidated
illustrious
incident
inherit
latitude
loath
maintain
renovate
reprimand
supervise

7. The team **comprises**
   (a) music in their heads and then writes it down later.
   (b) a dozen players.
   (c) people of all races, genders, and religions.
   (d) every time they lose a game.

8. The **supervisor**
   (a) was satisfied with the quality of the food.
   (b) made sure they got to work on time.
   (c) of the project claimed to be happy with the progress so far.
   (d) needed to be turned off before it overheated.

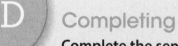

Completing Sentences

Complete the sentences to demonstrate your knowledge of the words in bold.

1. One way to **correspond** is by

   _____.

2. An **illustrious** person I know of is

   _____.

3. From my ancestors I **inherited**

   _____.

4. A recent **acquisition** of mine is

   _____.

5. I should be given more **latitude** because

   _____.

6. I feel **competent** to

   _____.

7. I would be **loath** to

   _____.

8. It is important to **maintain**

   _____.

9. When you are **reprimanded,** that means you

   _____.

10. My gym outfit **comprises**

   _____.

Mount Vernon

No visit to Washington, D.C., is complete without a trip to Mount Vernon, the **illustrious** home of George Washington, our nation's first president. It is located just a few miles south of our nation's capital. Its expansive views, spacious lawns, shaded walks, and carefully manicured gardens make it one of the most popular tourist attractions in the nation. More than a million people annually visit Mount Vernon. There they may pay respects to the memory of our first president and his wife, the first lady; both are buried there.

Mount Vernon had been in the Washington family for almost a hundred years when George Washington **inherited** the property in 1761. It **comprised** five separate farms as well as the main residence overlooking the Potomac River, which he occupied with his wife and her two children from a former marriage. Because the house was too small for their needs, Washington added rooms and outbuildings. Some of this work was completed by the 317 enslaved people Washington kept at Mount Vernon. He also hired paid workers and **supervised** their work closely; by the time they had finished, Mount Vernon had been transformed into the fine mansion visitors see today.

Washington was **loath** to leave his beautiful home. But his duty to his country required him to be absent from Mount Vernon from 1775 until 1783. During that time he commanded the Continental army in the war against the British. In his absence, a distant cousin, Lund Washington, managed the property for him. We know a great deal about this period in the history of Mount Vernon because the abundant **correspondence** between the two men has survived.

Washington gave his cousin considerable **latitude** in looking after the estate, and Lund was a **competent** manager. However, one **incident** aroused Washington's wrath. Lund informed him that a British warship had navigated up the river, and the crew had asked for food. Lund had not wanted to **antagonize** them and had complied with their request. Washington **reprimanded** his cousin, telling him that he should have refused to accommodate the British "even if they had burned my house and laid the Plantation in ruins."

acquire
antagonize
competent
comprise
correspond
dilapidated
illustrious
incident
inherit
latitude
loath
maintain
renovate
reprimand
supervise

In 1789, Washington reluctantly left Mount Vernon once again to serve as the country's first president. After eight years he retired from public life and returned for the last time to his beloved home. Two years later he died. The property remained in the Washington family until 1858. By then, the house was in a sadly **dilapidated** state. In that year, the Mount Vernon Ladies Association, an organization of private citizens, **acquired** the property. The association carefully **renovated** the house. It now looks as it did when George Washington lived there. The Mount Vernon Ladies Association has **maintained** it ever since and makes it available to the public to view every day of the year.

▶ **Answer each of the following questions with a sentence. If a question does not contain a vocabulary word from the lesson's word list, use one in your answer. Use each word only once.**

1. What is the meaning of **latitude** as it is used in the passage?

_____

_____

2. Who **supervised** the workers at Mount Vernon between 1775 and 1783?

_____

_____

3. Was George Washington eager to leave Mount Vernon in 1789?

_____

_____

4. Why does Washington have a secure place in United States history?

_____

_____

5. Why did George Washington, on the whole, have reason to be satisfied with his cousin's management?

_____

_____

6. Was George Washington at Mount Vernon when the British warship arrived?

_____

_____

7. Was George Washington pleased when his cousin helped the British?

_____

_____

8. What is the meaning of **comprised** as it is used in the passage?

_____

_____

9. How did George Washington know what was going on at Mount Vernon while he was away?

_____

_____

10. Why did Lund give the British what they asked for?

_____

_____

11. What is the meaning of **inherited** as it is used in the passage?

_____

_____

12. Had the Washington family taken good care of Mount Vernon prior to its purchase by the Mount Vernon Ladies Association?

_____

_____

13. What was Mount Vernon in need of in 1858?

_____

_____

14. In what year did George Washington become the owner of Mount Vernon?

_____

_____

15. What is the meaning of **maintained** as it is used in the passage?

_____

_____

| acquire |
| antagonize |
| competent |
| comprise |
| correspond |
| dilapidated |
| illustrious |
| incident |
| inherit |
| latitude |
| loath |
| maintain |
| renovate |
| reprimand |
| supervise |

Fun & Fascinating FACTS

- *Inheritance* is a noun related to the word list's first meaning of the verb **inherit.** An *inheritance* is the property received from a person after her or his death. Another noun that relates to the first meaning of *inherit* is *heir,* one who *inherits* property. *Heredity* is another noun related to the second meaning of *inherit. Heredity* is the passing on from parents to children of the things that make up that person, both physically and mentally.

- Lines of **latitude** are imaginary lines parallel to and north and south of the equator. *Latitudes* close to zero degrees are near the equator; *latitudes* close to 90 degrees are near the poles. Lines of *longitude* run from pole to pole and are measured east and west of Greenwich, England. (The *latitude* of Los Angeles is 34 degrees north; its *longitude* is 118 degrees west.)

- The Latin for *new* is *novus,* which forms the root of the verb **renovate.** Other words formed from this root include *novice,* "a person new to an activity" (a tennis *novice*); *novelty,* "something that excites interest because it is new" (a popular *novelty* in the stores this holiday season); and *innovation,* "a new way of doing something" (the latest *innovation* in the automobile industry).

maintain

verb 1. To continue in the same way or condition; stay the same.

2. To insist that something is true.

*The walkers try to **maintain** an even pace as they exercise.*

Academic Context

It is not difficult to **maintain** excellent grades throughout school. It just takes a bit of effort.

Context Clues

These sentences give clues to the meaning of **maintain.**

> *When biking in a hilly area, it's difficult to **maintain** a constant speed.*
> *Sasha **maintains** that it was her little brother who spilled the juice on the floor.*

Discussion & Writing Prompt

What are some things a person can do to **maintain** excellent health?

2 min.	3 min.
1. Turn and talk to your partner or group.	**2.** Write 2–4 sentences.
Use this space to take notes or draw your ideas.	Be ready to share what you have written.

Review

Crossword Puzzle   Solve the crossword puzzle by studying the clues and filling in the answer boxes. The number after a clue is the lesson the word is from.

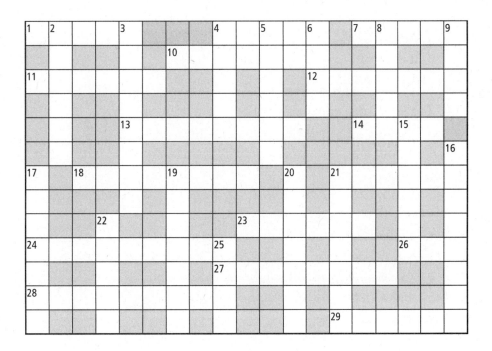

Clues Across

1. To become weaker; to decrease **(1)**
7. Forceful anger; fury **(3)**
10. Something that exists only in the mind **(2)**
11. Wise in a clever or practical way **(2)**
12. To gain ownership **(4)**
13. To keep in good condition **(4)**
14. Something fake or false **(1)**
18. Imaginary; not real **(2)**
21. A deadly disease that spreads rapidly **(3)**
23. To eat up hungrily **(2)**
24. Having the ability to do what is needed **(4)**
26. Comes before D E F
27. To make like new again **(4)**
28. To direct or manage activities **(4)**
29. Eight multiplied by ten

Clues Down

2. To present as a gift **(3)**
3. To figure out roughly **(1)**
4. Something that brings about a result **(1)**
5. Lacking; empty **(3)**
6. A luminous body in the night sky
8. Opposite of *smooth*
9. To pay attention to **(3)**
15. A large country in central Africa
16. A choice item of food **(2)**
17. Exact; specific **(1)**
19. To receive after the death of someone **(4)**
20. Not frank or honest **(3)**
21. Birds' feathers **(2)**
22. Excessive _____ on the highway can kill.
25. A long, slow, and difficult journey **(1)**

Study the definitions of the words. Then do the exercises that follow.

adequate
ad´ ə kwət

adj. Enough; sufficient.
One blanket will be **adequate** on such a warm night.

Talk to your partner about whether a glass of water is adequate when you're thirsty.

administer
ad min´ is tər

v. 1. To manage or direct.
The Red Cross **administers** the blood donor program.

2. To give out as treatment or assistance.
The scout leader **administered** first aid to the child who had cut his hand.

Discuss with your partner who administered the most recent test you took.

agitate
aj´ ə tāt

v. 1. To disturb or upset.
Talk of sharks in the water **agitated** swimmers at the beach.

2. To move with an irregular, fast, or violent action.
Strong winds **agitated** the surface of the lake.

3. To stir up interest in and support for a cause.
The miners **agitated** for better working conditions.

Chat with your partner about a person who agitated for civil rights.

capitulate
kə pich´ yōō lāt

v. To give in; to surrender.
The school board **capitulated** to the students' demands and changed the dress-code policy.

citrus
si´ trəs

n. 1. A fruit of the family that includes oranges, lemons, grapefruits, and limes.
A **citrus** is an excellent source of vitamin C.

2. A tree that produces these fruits.
Citruses grow well in Florida.

adj. Of or relating to these fruits or trees.
The kumquat is a less well-known member of the **citrus** family.

disrupt
dis rupt′

v. 1. To break up the orderly course of.
Angry protesters **disrupted** the president's speech.

2. To interrupt; to bring to a temporary halt.
A strike by the drivers **disrupted** service on the subway.

disruptive *adj.* Causing confusion or disorder.
Disruptive behavior is not acceptable in the classroom.

disruption *n.* A disturbance that interrupts or causes confusion.
Work on the cell towers caused a temporary **disruption** of service.

....

Talk to your partner about the best way for teachers to handle classroom disruptions.

hovel
huv′ əl

n. An unpleasant, cramped, and dilapidated place to live.
In the eleventh century, the Saxons complained that they were forced to live in **hovels,** while their Norman conquerers had fine homes.

illiterate
il lit′ ər ət

adj. Unable to read or write.
Volunteers are needed to help teach **illiterate** adults how to read.

illiteracy *n.* Inability to read or write.
Illiteracy is practically nonexistent in Japan.

indifferent
in dif′ ər ənt

adj. 1. Not concerned about; not caring.
The authorities can no longer afford to be **indifferent** to the problem of nuclear-waste disposal.

2. Neither very good nor very bad; passable.
Her **indifferent** grades in school worried her parents.

....

Demonstrate how you might act indifferent to your partner.

menial
mē′ nē əl

adj. Of or relating to low-level, humble work.
Oliver accepted **menial** work with low pay, because he was glad to have a job.

permanent
pʉr′ mə nənt

adj. Lasting or expected to last for a long time.
A child's first **permanent** teeth appear at about the age of six.

....

Exchange ideas with your partner about whether you think humans will ever have a permanent home on another planet.

respite
res′ pit

n. A period of rest; a pause.
The rain brought a welcome **respite** from the tremendous heat.

strenuous
stren′ yo͞o əs

adj. 1. Needing much effort; using a lot of energy.
Chopping wood is **strenuous** work.

2. Very active; vigorous.
The plan to close the local school met with **strenuous** opposition from parents.

toil toil	*v.* 1. To work long and hard. Sugarcane cutters **toil** in the fields from dawn to dusk. 2. To make one's way with difficulty. We **toiled** up the steep hill. *n.* Hard and tiring labor. After a lifetime of **toil,** my grandmother is ready to enjoy her retirement.
urgent ʉr´jənt	*adj.* Needing quick action or attention. The county has an **urgent** need for a new hospital. **urgency** *n.* The need for quick action. The senator stressed the **urgency** of cleaning up the polluted waters of our country. *Discuss with your partner something your school has an urgent need of.*

5A Finding Meanings

Choose two phrases to form a sentence that correctly uses a word from Word List 5. Then write the sentence.

adequate
administer
agitate
capitulate
citrus
disrupt
hovel
illiterate
indifferent
menial
permanent
respite
strenuous
toil
urgent

1. (a) work long and hard.   (c) To toil is to
   (b) To capitulate is to   (d) move with an irregular, violent action.

   _____

   _____

2. (a) that can be taken two ways.   (c) that is expressed with force.
   (b) A strenuous response is one   (d) An indifferent response is one

   _____

   _____

3. (a) Illiteracy is   (c) the inability to read or write.
   (b) Urgency is   (d) an unwillingness to be concerned.

   _____

   _____

4. (a) a building to house animals.   (c) A hovel is
   (b) A respite is   (d) a small and dilapidated house.

   _____

   _____

5. (a) avoid the company of others.　　(c) To be indifferent is to
   (b) be merely passable.　　　　　　(d) To be permanent is to

   _____

   _____

6. (a) To agitate　　　　　　　　　(c) is to surrender.
   (b) is to become bold or brave.　　(d) To capitulate

   _____

   _____

7. (a) seems worse than it really is.　(c) A permanent problem is one that
   (b) requires attention right away.　(d) An urgent problem is one that

   _____

   _____

8. (a) To disrupt a program is to　　(c) be responsible for running it.
   (b) To administer a program is to　(d) provide the money for it.

   _____

   _____

9. (a) A respite is　　　　　　　　(c) a lemon or similar fruit.
   (b) A citrus is　　　　　　　　　(d) a task requiring hard work.

   _____

   _____

10. (a) that person is disturbed or upset.　(c) If someone is agitated,
    (b) that person avoids other people.　(d) If someone is disruptive,

   _____

   _____

5B Just the Right Word

Replace each phrase in bold with a single word (or form of the word) from the word list.

1. Although entry-level jobs may seem **low level and humble,** young people can still take pride in them and do them to the best of their ability.

2. Political protesters **stirred up** the crowd with their loud, expressive language.

3. The one-room apartment was **just large enough** for one person.

4. The work of a logger is **tiring because it requires a lot of effort.**

5. The man who was **causing a disturbance** during the performance was asked to be quiet.

6. I'm afraid that this ink stain is **not going to go away.**

7. Although I asked him for help repeatedly, he was **not interested in listening** to my requests.

8. We worked in the garden all afternoon without a **break from our activity.**

9. What an unpleasant task it was to **make my way with difficulty** through five hundred pages of small print.

10. This medicine must be **given to the patient** by a nurse or doctor.

5C Applying Meanings

Circle the letter or letters next to each correct answer. There may be more than one correct answer.

adequate
administer
agitate
capitulate
citrus
disrupt
hovel
illiterate
indifferent
menial
permanent
respite
strenuous
toil
urgent

1. Which of the following would be a matter of **urgency?**
   (a) a fire
   (b) a sudden epidemic
   (c) a hurricane warning
   (d) an overdue library book

2. Which of the following can become **agitated?**
   (a) water
   (b) a crowd
   (c) a rock
   (d) a child

3. Which of the following is a **citrus** fruit?
   (a) a grapefruit
   (b) an avocado
   (c) an orange
   (d) a banana

4. Which of the following might an **illiterate** person do?
   (a) play checkers
   (b) write a report
   (c) solve a crossword puzzle
   (d) play a word game

5. Which of the following can **capitulate?**
   (a) an army
   (b) a country
   (c) a person
   (d) a building

6. Which of the following is a **strenuous** activity?
   (a) shoveling snow
   (c) washing dishes
   (b) swimming
   (d) taking a stroll

7. Which of the following can be **disrupted?**
   (a) a speech
   (c) one's education
   (b) a meeting
   (d) one's vacation

8. Which of the following is an **adequate** grade?
   (a) A-
   (c) B
   (b) C+
   (d) F

Word Study: Analogies

Complete the analogies by selecting the pair of words whose relationship most resembles the relationship of the pair in capital letters. Circle the letter next to the pair you choose.

1. INCREASE : SUBSIDE ::
   (a) praise : flatter
   (c) lessen : abate
   (b) guess : estimate
   (d) expand : contract

2. ILLITERATE : READ ::
   (a) immortal : die
   (c) urgent : urge
   (b) dilapidated : renovate
   (d) tired : stumble

3. SURRENDER : CAPITULATE ::
   (a) heed : annihilate
   (c) arrive : depart
   (b) rest : toil
   (d) gain : acquire

4. UPSET : AGHAST ::
   (a) mortal : immortal
   (c) hungry : thirsty
   (b) genuine : authentic
   (d) tired : exhausted

5. HEED : IGNORE ::
   (a) lend : debt
   (c) accept : reject
   (b) disturb : agitate
   (d) maintain : declare

6. HOVEL : PALACE ::
   (a) hut : shelter
   (c) money : health
   (b) king : queen
   (d) poverty : wealth

7. LEMON : CITRUS ::
   (a) apple : orange
   (c) letter : package
   (b) wheat : grain
   (d) plant : animal

8. TOIL : TIRED ::
   - (a) devour : full
   - (b) judging : impartial
   - (c) hiking : devious
   - (d) supplies : adequate

9. REPRIMAND : PRAISE ::
   - (a) disrupt : interrupt
   - (b) correspond : match
   - (c) surrender : capitulate
   - (d) insult : flatter

10. PERMANENT : TEMPORARY ::
   - (a) astute : clever
   - (b) abbreviated : brief
   - (c) competent : able
   - (d) industrious : lazy

5E Vocabulary in Context
Read the passage.

Harvest of Shame

Many Americans are lucky to have access to ample supplies of fruits and vegetables in their supermarkets twelve months a year. And who harvests all this food? More than a million women, children, and men do. They crisscross the United States picking asparagus and strawberries in Washington State, **citrus** fruits in Florida, apples in New York State, and a host of different fruits and vegetables in California. These laborers are called migrant farmworkers because they move from place to place, wherever crops need picking. Most would prefer **permanent** full-time employment, but it is not often available to them.

The workday is **strenuous;** pickers bend and stoop, often under a blazing hot sun. And the day is exceptionally long—from seven in the morning until seven at night. Their only **respite** may be a twenty-minute lunch break. It is considered **menial** work; wages are low, and laborers are paid only when they pick. If it rains, or if they are too sick to work, they get nothing. What's more, they often have difficulty obtaining **adequate** medical treatment when they are ill or injured.

The children suffer enormous disadvantages because their education is **disrupted** as they move from school to school. In fact, only one student in ten graduates from high school. Young people often drop out of school altogether to **toil** in the fields alongside their parents. It is there that they may be exposed to the chemical pesticides that are routinely sprayed on crops. One California

adequate
administer
agitate
capitulate
citrus
disrupt
hovel
illiterate
indifferent
menial
permanent
respite
strenuous
toil
urgent

study demonstrated that the cancer rate among migrant workers' children was twelve times the national average rate.

In the 1960s, laborers in California began to **agitate** for more progressive working conditions. The growers were **indifferent** to their demands. So the migrant workers, under the leadership of two Mexican Americans, Cesar Chavez and Dolores Fernandez Huerta, formed a labor union called the United Farm Workers of America. When growers tried to oppose the union, it called strikes and organized boycotts of California lettuce and grapes. There were years of struggle, many organized marches, and sometimes violent clashes, but in the end the majority of growers **capitulated.** In 1966, they recognized the union's right to represent workers.

Despite the union's efforts, conditions have improved minimally since the 1960s. One notable accomplishment has been the creation of the East Coast Migrant Head Start Project, which **administers** many childcare centers for migrants. Started in 1974, it now serves over three thousand children annually along the East Coast. Motivation, Education & Training (MET) is a similar program that helps migrant workers in five states. Though these programs have helped improve conditions in some areas, the need for additional programs is **urgent.** Educational programs could lower **illiteracy** rates among migrant workers and their families, while outreach programs could help improve migrant workers' living conditions. Many workers survive without running water or electricity. These necessary additions and repairs to homes would help convert them from inadequate **hovels** into acceptable community housing.

In 1960, a CBS documentary film about migrant workers aired on television the day after Thanksgiving. It brought into people's homes the truth about how the nation's crops were harvested, and it shocked the nation. Fifty years later, in 2010, CBS television broadcast a program to mark the occasion. It showed that while there had been some improvement in wages and working conditions, much remains to be done. The name of the documentary film is *Harvest of Shame*.

▶ **Answer each of the following questions with a sentence. If a question does not contain a vocabulary word from the lesson's word list, use one in your answer. Use each word only once.**

1. What is the meaning of **strenuous** as it is used in the passage?

_____

_____

2. What do oranges, grapefruit, and lemons have in common?

_____

_____

3. What is the meaning of **administers** as it is used in the passage?

_____

_____

4. Describe the living conditions of many migrant farmworkers.

_____

_____

5. In what ways did the union **agitate** for better conditions?

_____

_____

6. Is there still much need to improve the conditions of migrant workers?

_____

_____

7. What is the meaning of **disrupted** as it is used in the passage?

_____

_____

8. Why do some consider this type of work **menial?**

_____

_____

9. What did farmworkers gain when the growers **capitulated** in 1966?

_____

_____

10. What is the meaning of **toil** as it is used in the passage?

_____

_____

11. How would **permanent** employment improve the state of migrant workers?

_____

_____

| adequate |
| administer |
| agitate |
| capitulate |
| citrus |
| disrupt |
| hovel |
| illiterate |
| indifferent |
| menial |
| permanent |
| respite |
| strenuous |
| toil |
| urgent |

12. Why is a twenty-minute lunch break especially welcome to farmworkers?

_____

_____

13. What is the meaning of **indifferent** as it is used in the passage?

_____

_____

14. Why is the produce section at supermarkets usually well stocked?

_____

_____

15. How could educational programs help the workers and their families?

_____

_____

Fun & Fascinating FACTS

- The noun formed from the verb **administer** is *administration*; its general meaning is "the management of a business," but it also has a specialized meaning, "the members of the executive branch of government, headed by the president." In this meaning, the word is usually capitalized. (During the Clinton *Administration*, Janet Reno became the first female Attorney General of the United States.) The other two branches of government are the legislative (the Senate and the House of Representatives) and the judicial (headed by the United States Supreme Court).

- The Latin word for *break* is *ruptura*; from this word, we form the verbs **disrupt** and *interrupt*. If you *interrupt* a speaker, you *break* in on what that person is saying. If you try to *disrupt* a meeting, you are attempting to *break* it up.

- The antonym of **illiterate** is *literate*. Its primary meaning is "able to read," but it has two secondary meanings: "well read" (a *literate* scholar), and "well written; polished" (a *literate* essay).

Vocabulary Extension

adequate

adjective Enough; sufficient.

Word Family

adequately (adverb)

in**adequate** (adjective)

in**adequate**ly (adverb)

Context Clues

These sentences give clues to the meaning of **adequate.**

> *The donation was more than **adequate** to cover the cost of the supplies for the project.*
>
> *If a plant does not receive an **adequate** amount of sunlight and water, it cannot grow.*

Discussion & Writing Prompt

How many hours of sleep do you feel is **adequate** for you? Explain your reasoning.

2 min.	3 min.
1. Turn and talk to your partner or group.	**2.** Write 2–4 sentences.
Use this space to take notes or draw your ideas.	Be ready to share what you have written.

Study the definitions of the words. Then do the exercises that follow.

addict
ad´ ikt

n. 1. A person with a very strong desire for something that is habit-forming and sometimes harmful.
Junk-food **addicts** can try to change their eating habits.

2. A person who is a very enthusiastic fan.
A true crossword-puzzle **addict** could complete this puzzle in twenty minutes.

v. (ə dikt´) To cause someone to have a very strong desire for something.
My grandmother succeeded in **addicting** me to her wonderful chocolate cake after making it for me so many times.

addiction   *n.* (ə dik´ shən) The condition of being addicted.
We need more treatment centers for drug **addiction.**

addictive   *adj.* (ə dik´ tiv) Likely to cause addiction.
Cigarettes contain **addictive** substances.

Tell your partner something you are an addict of, such as a computer game or a type of music.

aspire
ə spīr´

v. To have a strong desire to get or do something; to seek.
Every NFL team **aspires** to win the Super Bowl.

aspiration   *n.* (as pər ā´ shən) A strong desire to achieve something; an ambition.
Jian Xiao sings in local clubs but has **aspirations** to be an opera singer.

Share one of your aspirations with your partner.

bias
bī´ əs

n. A preference that prevents one from being impartial; prejudice.
The lawyers in town insist that Judge Lewis shows **bias** in favor of women.

v. To cause someone to have prejudice; to influence.
Don't let a single bad experience with one restaurant **bias** you against all others.

Talk to your partner about what a person can do when faced with bias because of race or gender.

blatant
blāt´ nt

adj. Very obvious in an offensive or shameless way.
Josiah's invitation to the entire class to come to his party was a **blatant** attempt to win votes in the student-council election.

candid
kan´ did

adj. Expressed honestly and without holding back unpleasant truths.
Tony asked the teacher for her **candid** opinion about his poem.

confront
kən frunt´

v. 1. To stand up to; to face boldly.
Do you intend to **confront** the people who have been spreading rumors about you?

2. To put or bring face-to-face.
When the police **confronted** the two suspects with the evidence, they confessed to the robbery.

confrontation   *n.* (kän frən tā´ shən) A hostile meeting between people who hold opposite views.
Rosie avoided a **confrontation** with her mother by staying in her room.

Discuss with your partner the best way to peacefully confront a bully.

debut
dā´ byōo

n. A first public appearance.
Radio broadcasting made its **debut** in 1920.

v. To make a first public appearance.
The new television shows **debut** in September.

enroll
en rōl´

v. To sign up to become a member of some group or activity; to register.
A scholarship made it possible for me to **enroll** in art school.

enrollment   *n.* The number of people enrolled.
The karate class has an **enrollment** of six students.

fluster
flus´ tər

v. To make nervous, embarrassed, or confused.
The question **flustered** me, so I was unable to think of an answer quickly.

impunity
im pyōo´ nə tē

n. Freedom from being harmed or punished.
Those who think they can litter with **impunity** are sadly mistaken.

intensify
in ten´ sə fī

v. To increase; to strengthen or deepen.
Volunteers will **intensify** their efforts to find the missing cat.

Explain to your partner what benefit might result if you intensify your study of vocabulary.

intimidate
in tim´ ə dāt

v. To frighten, especially by threatening someone.
The pitcher's scowl was intended to **intimidate** the batter.

intimidation   *n.* (in tim ə dā´ shən) The act of intimidating.
Kareem claimed that **intimidation** had been used to make him leave the park.

Chat with your partner about whether intimidation is the right way to influence people.

obnoxious
äb näk´ shəs

adj. Very unpleasant; disgusting.
An **obnoxious** diner at the next table ruined our meal by complaining in a very loud voice.

retort	*v.* To answer, especially in a quick or clever way.
rē tôrt´	"Spiders are afraid of *me*," I **retorted** when my friend said I was afraid of spiders.
	n. A quick or clever reply.
	Unable to think of a suitable **retort,** I remained silent.

Pretend to argue with your partner and see who can think of the funniest retort.

stint	*n.* 1. A period of time devoted to a job or some task.
stint	After finishing college, Catalina had a two-year **stint** in the Peace Corps in Kenya.
	2. A limit or restriction.
	Local benefactors gave without **stint** to help make the youth center a reality.
	v. To limit or restrict.
	Many parents **stint** on things they need to pay for their children's education.

6A Using Words in Context

Read the following sentences. If the word in bold is used correctly, write C on the line. If the word is used incorrectly, write I on the line.

1. (a) The clown came in on **stints,** making him look twelve feet tall. ___
   (b) Some people **stint** on things they need to pay for a vacation. ___
   (c) After a four-year **stint** in the army, Adeline went into banking. ___
   (d) Our group raised a **stint** of money for the local girls' club. ___

2. (a) "I've heard enough," Zara **retorted.** "Talk about something else." ___
   (b) Gabriel raised his voice to give his **retort** more force. ___
   (c) Jo tried to think of a **retort** that would make her friends laugh. ___
   (d) It was **retorted** in the newspapers that the president was coming to town. ___

3. (a) People can be **biased** when judging others. ___
   (b) The **bias** of the statue was made of marble. ___
   (c) The writer shows a strong **bias** in favor of a longer summer vacation. ___
   (d) There is no **bias** that the Yellowstone volcano is about to erupt. ___

4. (a) At the **debut** of the race, Isimu took the lead. ___
   (b) The dog food **debuted** on television in a sixty-second commercial. ___
   (c) Charlie Chaplin made his movie **debut** in 1914. ___
   (d) The top of the mountain was covered in a chilly **debut.** ___

5. (a) The lawyer did everything she could to **fluster** the witness. ___
   (b) Kateri got so **flustered,** he couldn't remember his own name. ___
   (c) The wind started to **fluster,** so we headed back to the house. ___
   (d) Sanjay's ball accidentally went over the fence, so we **flustered** it. ___

6. (a) The criminals felt they could break the law with **impunity.** ___
   (b) My cousin has climbed mountains with **impunity** for twenty years. ___
   (c) Some people have a natural **impunity** to certain diseases. ___
   (d) Yuan's **impunity** makes him hungry all the time. ___

7. (a) It is time to **confront** the problems with the library budget. ___
   (b) Calcium in high **confrontations** was discovered in the city water supply. ___
   (c) The teacher **confronted** the students and ordered them to behave. ___
   (d) The **confrontation** between Cal and Keiko ended peacefully. ___

8. (a) We learned **addiction** and subtraction in elementary school. ___
   (b) Playing video games can be seriously **addictive.** ___
   (c) Juana is **addicted** to novels set in the Middle Ages. ___
   (d) **Addiction** can be successfully treated. ___

9. (a) Bullies get their way by **intimidating** others. ___
   (b) The settlers were not supposed to **intimidate** with the local tribesmen. ___
   (c) **Intimidation** can be used to threaten someone. ___
   (d) If it's not an **intimidation,** it must be real. ___

10. (a) The boy **aspired** heavily as he hauled the boxes. ___
    (b) Zion **aspired** to be on the Supreme Court someday. ___
    (c) Her **aspirations** were shattered when she failed to get into drama school. ___
    (d) Kiara took a towel and wiped the **aspiration** from her brow. ___

addict
aspire
bias
blatant
candid
confront
debut
enroll
fluster
impunity
intensify
intimidate
obnoxious
retort
stint

Making Connections

Circle the letter next to each correct answer. There may be more than one correct answer.

1. Which word or words go with *increase?*
   (a) aspire   (b) intensify   (c) inflate   (d) annoy

2. Which word or words go with *unpleasant?*
   (a) candid   (b) detestable   (c) debut   (d) obnoxious

3. Which word or words go with *obvious?*
   (a) illustrious   (b) blatant   (c) competent   (d) ravenous

4. Which word or words go with *honest?*
   (a) candid   (b) incredible   (c) biased   (d) dilapidated

5. Which word or words go with *sign up?*
   (a) inherit   (b) fluster   (c) retort   (d) enroll

6. Which word or words go with *prejudice?*
   (a) debut   (b) bias   (c) impunity   (d) stint

7. Which word or words go with *frighten?*
   (a) intimidate   (b) enroll   (c) retort   (d) threaten

8. Which word or words go with *ambition?*
   (a) renovate   (b) aspire   (c) retort   (d) acquire

9. Which word or words go with *freedom from punishment?*
   (a) impunity   (b) devoid   (c) pardon   (d) stint

10. Which word or words go with *confused?*
    (a) competent   (b) flustered   (c) enrolled   (d) maintained

1. We **confronted**
   (a) each other across the chess board.
   (b) the problem and found a solution.
   (c) the American Revolution in 1776.
   (d) our way around the world in a few hours.

2. The **blatant**
   (a) disregard of school rules will not go unpunished.
   (b) sound of bells echoed across the valley.
   (c) lie was very obvious.
   (d) taste of the strawberries was delicious.

3. **Enrollment**
   (a) might be the best time to feed the dog.
   (b) for high school begins in ninth grade.
   (c) in poetry often rhymes.
   (d) for the little league team is open to everyone.

4. We **intensified**
   (a) the dog and decided she was okay.
   (b) our efforts to raise money for the project.
   (c) the colors to make them stand out.
   (d) to what happened this morning.

5. A **candid**
   (a) comment can hurt a person's feelings.
   (b) piece of advice may be just what is needed.
   (c) apple on a stick is a treat at the county fair.
   (d) suit made Jayden stand out from the crowd.

6. An **obnoxious**
   (a) passenger sat next to me on the bus and never stopped talking.
   (b) asteroid struck the earth sixty-five million years ago.
   (c) and ugly weed is spreading rapidly over the sidewalk.
   (d) remark was enough to get Felix shunned by the other guests.

addict
aspire
bias
blatant
candid
confront
debut
enroll
fluster
impunity
intensify
intimidate
obnoxious
retort
stint

7. A **stint**
   (a) of complaints followed Diego wherever he went.
   (b) in the Coast Guard was the high point of her life.
   (c) of honey in the cereal makes it taste so much better.
   (d) in the bakery with her mom made Lea want to go to culinary school.

8. I was **flustered**
   (a) to the concert in a taxi.
   (b) into writing the report.
   (c) when I thought my purse had been stolen.
   (d) after the teacher threw so many questions at me.

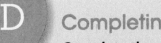

6D Completing Sentences

Complete the sentences to demonstrate your knowledge of the words in bold.

1. I might **confront** someone if

   _____ .

2. I **aspire** to

   _____ .

3. I get **flustered** when

   _____ .

4. You respond to someone with a **retort** when

   _____ .

5. A food I am **addicted** to is

   _____ .

6. I admit I am **biased** about

   _____ .

7. A habit I find **obnoxious** is

   _____ .

8. It's not nice to **intimidate** people because

   _____ .

9. At some point in my life I would like to do a **stint** as

   _____ .

10. If you say something **candidly,** that means you

   _____ .

Out of Her League?

Pam Postema grew up in Willard, Ohio, hooked on sports and with an unusual ambition—she **aspired** to be a major-league baseball umpire. At the time, this seemed like an impossible dream. No one took her seriously. Postema persisted, however, and in 1977 **enrolled** in the country's top umpiring school. At that time, she was twenty-two and well aware of the strong **bias** against women in professional baseball. Although the school she chose to attend had previously accepted several women, none had completed the course. In its entire history, the school had graduated seven thousand men but not one woman!

The umpiring school's chief instructor treated Postema fairly, and he was also very **candid** with her. He told her that her chances of getting a top job in the future were slim. In order to make it into the major leagues, she would have to be twice as good as any man. Postema was determined to succeed, and she did well at the school, graduating seventeenth out of a class of over a hundred students. She began at once to look for a job as a professional baseball umpire.

Within a few months, Postema made her professional **debut** with the Gulf Coast Single A League. During the next few years, she advanced steadily. In 1983, she began calling plays in the Triple A Pacific League, one step below the majors. It was not easy, though. If a male umpire made a bad call, it was brushed aside. If Postema did the same thing, she was accused of becoming **flustered.** Some baseball fans seized on any errors she made as "proof" that umpiring was not an appropriate occupation for a woman.

Postema believed that a manager would often view a **confrontation** with her as a test of his manhood; if he failed to **intimidate** her, he felt somehow disgraced. She wanted to show that no one should expect to attack her authority with **impunity,** so she ejected managers and players from the game at twice the rate of other umpires. She even had three spectators thrown out of the ballpark for making **obnoxious** remarks about female umpires. Postema admits she sometimes enjoyed arguing, whether with managers, players, or even other umpires. In fact, she says that many umpires are **addicted** to arguing.

In 1988, Postema got a job umpiring the National League spring-training games, where she had to deal with major-league players and managers. When the starting pitcher for the Pittsburgh Pirates told a reporter that God never

addict
aspire
bias
blatant
candid
confront
debut
enroll
fluster
impunity
intensify
intimidate
obnoxious
retort
stint

intended women to be major-league baseball umpires, Postema **retorted** that she doubted that God was interested in baseball. Not everyone was as **blatant** as the Pirates' pitcher. But the hostility directed against her, far from diminishing, seemed to **intensify** as her career advanced.

Pam Postema's career as a professional baseball umpire was marked by talent and spirit. Her **stint** in the minors had lasted seven years when she was dropped from the official list of umpires. There was nothing unusual about this. After about five years in the minors, most umpires are let go to give others a chance; very few make it into the majors. Did Pam Postema fail? Let's ask Ria Cortesio. In 2007, eighteen years after Pam retired from the game, Ria became the second woman to umpire a spring training game. She was the first to give credit to Pam Postema for leading the way.

▶ **Answer each of the following questions with a sentence. If a question does not contain a vocabulary word from the lesson's word list, use one in your answer. Use each word only once.**

1. When did Pam Postema make her first professional public appearance in a major-league game?

_____

_____

2. Did Postema fulfill her chief **aspiration?**

_____

_____

3. How did Postema show that managers could not easily **intimidate** her?

_____

_____

4. According to Postema, what habit is often common in umpires?

_____

_____

5. Why was it especially important for Postema not to get **flustered?**

_____

_____

6. How did three fans learn early on that they couldn't insult Postema with **impunity?**

_____

_____

7. What happens to most minor-league umpires?

_____

_____

8. Why might Postema have had reason to respect her instructor's predictions about her future in the major leagues?

_____

_____

9. Was Postema the first woman to attend the umpiring school?

_____

_____

10. How did the Pirates' pitcher show his **bias?**

_____

_____

11. Was the remark of the Pirates' pitcher typical of other pitchers as well?

_____

_____

12. How did Postema feel about sexist remarks from spectators?

_____

_____

13. Who had the last word in the argument between Postema and the Pirates' pitcher?

_____

_____

14. According to Postema, why did managers often make life difficult for her?

_____

_____

| addict |
| aspire |
| bias |
| blatant |
| candid |
| confront |
| debut |
| enroll |
| fluster |
| impunity |
| intensify |
| intimidate |
| obnoxious |
| retort |
| stint |

15. How did Postema demonstrate that she was not a quitter?

_____

_____

Fun & Fascinating FACTS

- The English word **candid** comes from the Latin verb *candere,* which means "to shine." Truth is like a light, sometimes exposing what someone might wish to hide. A *candid* person shines the light of truth on something others might wish to conceal.

- The Latin verb *punire* means "to punish" and forms the root of several other English words besides *punish* and **impunity.** If a jury awards *punitive* damages to someone who has been injured, the intention is to punish those who caused the injury. If you pay a *penalty,* you are being punished for doing what you shouldn't have done or for failing to do what you should have done. A state's *penal* system is designed to punish criminals by putting them in jail.

- **Obnoxious** is formed from the Latin *noxa,* meaning "an injury"; so is *noxious,* meaning "harmful" or "unhealthy" (*noxious* gas from car exhaust). The smell from a skunk is *obnoxious* but not *noxious.* Carbon monoxide gas is *noxious* but not *obnoxious* (because it cannot be smelled).

intensify

verb To increase; to strengthen or deepen.

*When the sun came out, the heat inside the car **intensified.***

Academic Context

If students choose to **intensify** their learning, they could receive college credit for certain classes.

Word Family

intense (adjective)

intensely (adverb)

intensified (adjective)

intensity (noun)

Discussion & Writing Prompt

Describe what happens when rainy weather **intensifies** into a storm.

2 min.	3 min.
1. Turn and talk to your partner or group.	**2.** Write 2–4 sentences.
Use this space to take notes or draw your ideas.	Be ready to share what you have written.

Study the definitions of the words. Then do the exercises that follow.

beseech
bē sēch´

v. To ask earnestly; to beg.
I **beseech** you to stay just one more day.

consternation
kän stər na´ shən

n. Amazement or fear that makes one feel confused.
We were filled with **consternation** when we saw that our car had been towed.

delectable
dē lek´ tə bəl

adj. Pleasing to the senses, especially to the sense of taste; delicious.
My grandfather's homemade apple pie is **delectable.**

garland
gär´ lənd

n. A wreath or chain of leaves and flowers.
The islanders greet new arrivals with **garlands** of fresh flowers to put around their necks.

gratify
grat´ i fī

v. 1. To please or satisfy.
The Red Cross was **gratified** by the response to its appeal for blood donors.

2. To give in to what is wanted or requested.
My parents were unable to **gratify** my wish for a pony.

gratifying *adj.* Pleasing.
It is **gratifying** to see one's hard work in math rewarded with higher grades.

....

Tell your partner if it is gratifying to see the smiles of people you help.

haughty
hôt´ ē

adj. Showing too much pride in oneself and scorn or contempt for others.
Sofia's **haughty** manner made her unpopular.

haughtiness *n.* The state or quality of being haughty.
His **haughtiness** seemed absurd for one who had accomplished so little.

....

Discuss with your partner whether a person who displays haughtiness will have many friends.

impetuous
im pech´ ōō əs

adj. Likely to act without thinking; hasty.
I regretted my **impetuous** decision to invite everyone at Marcello's party to come over to my place.

lavish
lav´ish

adj. 1. Much more than enough.
The Chinese New Year's celebration included a **lavish** fifteen-course meal.

2. Very costly.
The tribal chiefs at the ceremony bestowed **lavish** gifts on each other as signs of respect.

v. To give freely or generously.
Critics **lavished** praise on the new Broadway musical.

Share with your partner something fun you would like to lavish your time on.

pluck
pluk

v. 1. To pull off or out; to pick.
I was tempted to **pluck** a rose from the bush, but the sight of the thorns stopped me.

2. To remove the feathers from.
The chef **plucked** the chicken before the meal.

3. To pull at and let go.
You play the harp by **plucking** the strings gently.

n. Courage; bravery.
It took a lot of **pluck** for Rico to learn to walk again.

plucky *adj.* Brave; courageous.
After a **plucky** attempt to rescue the kitten stuck in the tree, Monique had to call the fire department.

Talk to your partner about a historical figure who displayed pluck, such as Rosa Parks.

ponder
pän´dər

v. To think about; to consider carefully.
Lost in thought, the chess player **pondered** her next move.

privilege
priv´ə lij

n. A special favor, right, or advantage given to a person or group.
Free parking at Reagan National Airport is one of the **privileges** enjoyed by members of Congress.

privileged *adj.* Given favors or advantages denied to others.
You should feel **privileged** that you were able to attend the glee-club competition in Chicago.

Chat with your partner about whether there are any privileges of being a teenager.

prostrate
präs´ trāt

adj. 1. Lying flat.
Having fainted, he lay **prostrate** on the floor.

2. Lying facedown, especially to show respect.
The worshippers in the temple lay **prostrate** before the priest.

3. Completely overcome; weak and helpless.
People were **prostrate** with terror as the tornado approached.

Share with your partner a time when you were prostrate with fear.

rapture
rap´ chər

n. A state of great joy, delight, or love.
The Scot was filled with **rapture** at the sound of bagpipes.

revelry
rev´ əl rē

n. Noisy merrymaking.
Sounds of **revelry** came from the locker room after the game.

whim
wim

n. A sudden wish to do something without a particular reason; a fanciful idea.
Purchasing a puppy is not something to be done on a **whim.**

Tell your partner about something you did on a whim. Was it a sensible thing to do?

7A

Finding Meanings

Choose two phrases to form a sentence that correctly uses a word from Word List 7. Then write the sentence.

1. (a) A plucky attempt is one
   (b) that takes a lot of courage.
   (c) An impetuous attempt is one
   (d) that is bound to fail.

   _____

   _____

2. (a) To be prostrate is to be
   (b) devoid of hope.
   (c) To be gratified is to be
   (d) lying with the face downward.

   _____

   _____

3. (a) To act impetuously is to
   (b) do something without thinking.
   (c) do something knowing it to be wrong.
   (d) To act in a haughty manner is to

   _____

   _____

4. (a) is to be watchful and alert.
   (b) is to be blissfully happy.
   (c) To be in a state of rapture
   (d) To be in a state of consternation

_____

_____

5. (a) A haughty person is
   (b) A privileged person is
   (c) one who tries to please others.
   (d) one who shows contempt for others.

_____

_____

6. (a) A whim is
   (b) a wreath of leaves and flowers.
   (c) A garland is
   (d) a small gift.

_____

_____

7. (a) Consternation is
   (b) contempt for the feelings
       of others.
   (c) Revelry is
   (d) a state of shocked surprise.

_____

_____

8. (a) To be prostrate is to be
   (b) To be gratified is to be
   (c) dissatisfied.
   (d) helpless.

_____

_____

9. (a) Pluck is
   (b) a display of joy.
   (c) noisy merrymaking.
   (d) Revelry is

_____

_____

10. (a) to give it freely.
    (b) To lavish something is
    (c) To ponder something is
    (d) to feel uncomfortable about it.

_____

_____

| beseech |
| consternation |
| delectable |
| garland |
| gratify |
| haughty |
| impetuous |
| lavish |
| pluck |
| ponder |
| privilege |
| prostrate |
| rapture |
| revelry |
| whim |

Just the Right Word

Replace each phrase in bold with a single word (or form of the word) from the word list.

1. I **am making an earnest request to** you not to get involved in their quarrel.

2. The **feeling of great joy and love** in the faces of the bride and groom was captured in the wedding photographs.

3. Imagine being able to buy a plane ticket to Tahiti on a **sudden wish to do something out of the ordinary!**

4. Parents do not have to **show they care by giving in to** every wish of their children.

5. I felt **that I was being given a special favor** when my parents let me go on a weekend trip with my friend and her family.

6. Getting back on a horse after taking a bad fall takes **a lot of courage.**

7. The student **gave a great deal of thought to** the question before replying.

8. The pizza at Saracino's is **pleasing to the taste.**

9. The new government offices are so **much more luxurious than is necessary** that reporters were shocked at the waste of money.

10. We were **lying stretched out flat on the ground** from fatigue after our hike.

7c Applying Meanings

Circle the letter or letters next to each correct answer. There may be more than one correct answer.

1. Which of the following can express **haughtiness?**
   - (a) a look
   - (b) an insult
   - (c) a retort
   - (d) an epidemic

2. Which of the following could be considered a **privilege?**
   - (a) receiving a reprimand
   - (b) doing homework
   - (c) staying up late
   - (d) paying taxes

3. Which of the following can be **plucked?**
   - (a) feathers
   - (b) flowers
   - (c) trees
   - (d) guitar strings

4. Which of the following might be a part of **revelry?**
   - (a) dancing
   - (b) music
   - (c) solitude
   - (d) laughter

5. Which of the following actions by children would **gratify** their parents?
   - (a) making derogatory remarks
   - (b) making astute comments
   - (c) cleaning up their rooms
   - (d) disrupting supper

6. Which of the following might cause **consternation?**
   - (a) losing the car keys
   - (b) losing a wallet
   - (c) failing a test
   - (d) getting stuck in traffic

7. Which of the following might a person **ponder?**
   - (a) a choice of college
   - (b) a choice of leader
   - (c) the origin of the universe
   - (d) braking to avoid an accident

8. Which of the following might be done on a **whim?**
   - (a) electing a president
   - (b) administering a test
   - (c) buying a new coat
   - (d) building a space station

beseech
consternation
delectable
garland
gratify
haughty
impetuous
lavish
pluck
ponder
privilege
prostrate
rapture
revelry
whim

Add the correct form of the prefix _in-_ to the words. Then write the letter of the definition that best fits each new word.

The most common meaning of the prefix _in-_ is "not" or "without." With this meaning, it turns a word into its opposite. For example, it turns _correct_ into _incorrect_. The prefix _in-_ can also act as an intensifier, making the word to which it is attached stronger or more emphatic.

To make certain words easier to say, the prefix changes to _im-_ before the letters _b_, _m_, and _p_. It changes to _il-_ before the letter _l_, and it changes to _ir-_ before the letter _r_.

1. _____precise   _____   a. neither good or bad

2. _____partial   _____   b. not regular

3. _____furiate   _____   c. not relevant

4. _____relevant   _____   d. not precise

5. _____capable   _____   e. very hasty

6. _____different   _____   f. not literate

7. _____lustrious   _____   g. not partial

8. _____petuous   _____   h. not capable

9. _____literate   _____   i. extremely outstanding

10. _____regular   _____   j. make very angry

The Midas Touch

It is sometimes said of people who are good at making money that everything they touch turns to gold. Such people are said to have the "Midas touch," an expression that comes from an ancient Greek myth.

The Greek god Dionysus was visiting Phrygia, now part of Turkey, when his companion Silenus wandered off and got lost, arriving some time later at the court of King Midas. He was exhausted, and he slipped off his donkey and fell asleep on the ground. When King Midas came upon him, he recognized Silenus at once and felt **privileged** to receive a visit from the friend of a god.

King Midas was determined to make his guest's stay a pleasant one. Midas's daughter presented Silenus with **garlands** made from flowers she herself had picked, and servants fell **prostrate** to the ground when he passed and rushed to obey his every **whim.** Musicians filled the air with sweet music wherever he went, and every night the king honored Silenus with a **lavish** banquet at which the most **delectable** dishes were served. In short, Midas did everything he could think of to **gratify** his guest. The **revelries** continued until Dionysus finally arrived in search of his companion.

Dionysus told Midas that in return for his kindness to Silenus, he could have anything he wanted. Now, King Midas loved gold almost as much as he loved his own daughter, so he did not stop to **ponder** Dionysus's offer. "Make everything I touch turn to gold," he said. When Dionysus suggested that Midas was being **impetuous,** the king **haughtily** rejected the suggestion. He was too proud to take advice from anyone, even a god. He refused to change his mind, so Dionysus granted him his wish.

Eager to try out his new power, King Midas rushed into the garden as soon as his visitors had left and **plucked** an apple from a tree. In an instant it turned to gold. The king was in a state of **rapture.** He called out to his daughter and flung his arms around her as he told her the good news. To his **consternation,** she instantly turned into a gold statue.

King Midas was aghast when he saw the consequences of his greed. He **beseeched** Dionysus to take back his gift. Dionysus agreed to do so, and he also restored the king's daughter to her human state. As for King Midas, he learned this important lesson: Be careful what you ask for; you might get it.

beseech
consternation
delectable
garland
gratify
haughty
impetuous
lavish
pluck
ponder
privilege
prostrate
rapture
revelry
whim

▶ **Answer each of the following questions with a sentence. If a question does not contain a vocabulary word from the lesson's word list, use one in your answer. Use each word only once.**

1. What is the meaning of **gratify** as it is used in the passage?

_____

_____

2. What brought Midas's **rapture** to an end?

_____

_____

3. Where do you think Midas's daughter placed the **garlands** she gave Silenus?

_____

_____

4. Why might Silenus have praised the chefs who worked for Midas?

_____

_____

5. What is the meaning of **prostrate** as it is used in the passage?

_____

_____

6. How did Midas react when Dionysus suggested that he be cautious?

_____

_____

7. How did Midas's mood change when he saw what he had done?

_____

_____

8. Why should Midas have **pondered** Dionysus's offer?

_____

_____

9. Why did Dionysus agree to take back his gift?

_____

_____

10. What is the meaning of **plucked** as it is used in the passage?

_____

_____

11. Why did Midas go to such trouble to entertain Silenus?

_____

_____

12. Why had Silenus no cause to complain about the service he received?

_____

_____

13. Why did Midas not give himself time to think over Dionysus's offer?

_____

_____

14. For how long did Midas entertain Silenus?

_____

_____

15. What is the meaning of **lavish** as it is used in the passage?

_____

_____

| beseech |
| consternation |
| delectable |
| garland |
| gratify |
| haughty |
| impetuous |
| lavish |
| pluck |
| ponder |
| privilege |
| prostrate |
| rapture |
| revelry |
| whim |

Fun & Fascinating FACTS

- The adjectives **prostrate** and *prone* both mean "lying with the face downward," but there is a difference between them that should be noted. *Prostrate* suggests either a show of respect or a state of helplessness. *Prone* is a more neutral term; it indicates bodily position and nothing more (lying *prone* in a bed). The antonym of *prone* is *supine;* it means "lying with the face upward."

- The Latin verb *rapere* means "to seize" and forms the root of several English words. To be in a state of **rapture** is to be seized by deep feelings of joy. The adjective *rapt* means "deeply absorbed." It is difficult to get the attention of people who are *rapt* in thought; it is as though their minds have been seized by thoughts that mentally disconnect them from what is going on around them. Finally, there is *raptor,* the name for a bird of prey that seizes small animals or fish in its talons and carries them off to eat later. Hawks and eagles are *raptors.*

- In the eighteenth and nineteenth centuries, *whim-wham* was the name for a fanciful or amusing object worn as an ornament or decoration. The origin of the term is unknown, but it became shortened to **whim,** and its meaning was broadened so that a *whim* came to mean "a fanciful or amusing idea." *Whimsy* is a related word; it means "a fanciful or amusing quality." (*Alice in Wonderland* by Lewis Carroll is filled with *whimsy.*) The adjective form of *whimsy* is *whimsical;* it means "marked by whimsy; amusing or fanciful." (A battery-powered fork for twirling spaghetti was one of the *whimsical* objects on display.)

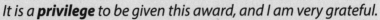

privilege

noun A special favor or advantage given to a person or a group.

*It is a **privilege** to be given this award, and I am very grateful.*

Context Clues

These sentences give clues to the meaning of **privilege.**

> *Students on the Honor Roll are given the **privilege** of skipping one day of school.*

> *Most students at the private school come from wealthy families who can afford the high tuition, but a few students are not as **privileged.***

Discussion & Writing Prompt

Do you think it's fair for a person to be given an advantage over others? When is it acceptable to enjoy a **privilege?**

2 min.	3 min.
1. Turn and talk to your partner or group.	**2.** Write 2–4 sentences.
Use this space to take notes or draw your ideas.	Be ready to share what you have written.

Study the definitions of the words. Then do the exercises that follow.

acrid
ak´ rid

adj. Sharp, irritating, or bitter to the sense of taste or smell.
Burning rubber gives off **acrid** fumes.

casualty
kazh´ ōō əl tē

n. A person killed or injured in a war or accident.
There were many **casualties** of the 2011 tsunami, or tidal wave, that struck Japan.

congested
kən jest´ əd

adj. 1. Overcrowded; filled too full.
We take the subway during rush hour to avoid the **congested** city streets.

2. Filled with fluid.
My sinuses get **congested** when the pollen count is high.

congestion *n.* 1. The condition of being overcrowded.
The **congestion** inside the furniture store is due to the "Going Out of Business" sale.

2. The condition of being filled with fluid.
Most cold remedies claim to relieve **congestion** for at least eight hours.

cope
kōp

v. To manage problems or difficulties successfully.
Extra police were on duty to **cope** with the large crowds expected for the parade.

Talk to your partner about how you cope in a stressful situation.

headlong
hed´ lôŋ

adj. With great speed or force; reckless.
The crowd made a **headlong** rush for the best seats as soon as the doors were opened.

adv. Recklessly; without time for careful thought.
It's foolish to rush **headlong** into a dispute that doesn't concern you.

hurtle
hərt´ l

v. To move with great force and speed.
A snowball **hurtled** past my ear.

impede
im pēd´

v. To get in the way of; to interfere with the movement of.
An overturned truck **impeded** the flow of traffic.

impediment *n.* (im ped´ ə mənt) An obstacle; something that gets in the way.
Poor roads are an **impediment** to travel.

Discuss with your partner what things impede you in the school hallways.

inevitable
in ev´ ə tə bəl

adj. Bound to happen; unavoidable.
A certain amount of wear on even the best tires is **inevitable** with normal use.

Tell your partner something about your life that is inevitable today.

initiate
i nish´ ē āt

v. 1. To put into effect; to bring into use.
The school **initiated** the new dress code on September 6.

2. To take in as a member.
The National Honor Society **initiated** thirty new members last evening.

initiation   *n.* (i nish ē ā´ shən) 1. The act of beginning.
The **initiation** of the new traffic plan has been delayed until the road is repaired.

2. The ceremony or process that makes one a member.
A celebration followed the **initiation** of new members into the San Francisco Film Society.

Chat with your partner about a new school rule you would like to initiate.

irate
ī rāt´

adj. Very angry; furious.
Irate citizens demanded that the chemical company stop polluting the lake.

lax
laks

adj. 1. Not strictly enforced; undemanding; careless.
Frequent inspections are designed to ensure that airline safety procedures have not become **lax.**

2. Not tight; loose.
When I felt the rope go **lax,** I knew that my partner had dropped the other end.

negligent
neg´ lə jənt

adj. Failing to take proper care of or to give proper attention to.
You were **negligent** when you failed to lock the car doors.

negligence   *n.* The quality, state, or act of being negligent.
When I went to camp, my houseplants died because of my sister's **negligence.**

Talk to your partner about what you should do if a friend displays negligence in the care of a pet.

smolder
smōl´ dər

v. 1. To burn slowly without bursting into flames.
Hot ashes **smolder** long after the flames of a campfire have died down.

2. To exist in a hidden state before bursting into the open.
A desire for freedom **smoldered** in the hearts of the people who left Cuba.

Share with your partner what feeling might smolder inside you if someone told you an exciting secret you couldn't tell anyone else.

stringent
strin´ jənt

adj. Strict; severe.
The **stringent** rules state that no exceptions can be made.

throng
thrôŋ

n. A large number of people gathered together; a crowd.
A **throng** of supporters cheered the president's arrival in Seattle.

v. To gather or move in large numbers.
Fans **thronged** into the ballpark for the first game of the World Series.

Tell your partner about a place where people throng.

8A Using Words in Context

Read the following sentences. If the word in bold is used correctly, write C on the line. If the word is used incorrectly, write I on the line.

1. (a) Food is **congested** through the mouth into the stomach. ___
   (b) Inhaling steam cleared my **congestion.** ___
   (c) The hermit avoided village life, finding it too **congested.** ___
   (d) It has been **congested** that Vikings came to America centuries before Columbus. ___

2. (a) The teacher thinks the hall monitor is too **lax** about enforcing the rules. ___
   (b) The line grew **lax,** and I knew the fish was off the hook. ___
   (c) To keep from falling off, keep a firm and **lax** hold on the bar. ___
   (d) Training had been **lax,** and that led to the accident. ___

3. (a) Elijah's complaints are as **inevitable** as frost in January. ___
   (b) They believe that a rise in oil prices is **inevitable.** ___
   (c) Was the fire **inevitable,** or could it have been prevented? ___
   (d) The depth of the water was too **inevitable** to be measured. ___

4. (a) The sun grew more **irate** as the clouds parted. ___
   (b) An **irate** customer demanded her money back. ___
   (c) **Irate** letters to the newspapers demanded an answer. ___
   (d) **Irate** parents insisted that the school be reopened. ___

5. (a) A **throng** of families gathered in the park for the farmer's market. ___
   (b) Wearing a multicolored **throng** is tradition on the island. ___
   (c) Visitors **thronged** the museum as soon as its doors opened. ___
   (d) A **throng** of runs in the ninth inning made the score 11 to 2. ___

6. (a) A fallen tree **impeded** access to the house. ___
   (b) The loss of a limb was no **impediment** to the determined athlete. ___
   (c) A speech **impediment** sometimes made it hard to understand Yasmeen. ___
   (d) The cattle suddenly **impeded** when thunder startled them. ___

7. (a) **Stringent** rules have now been put in place. ___
   (b) Track runners need to keep a **stringent** watch on the clock. ___
   (c) **Stringent** new speed limits reduced the number of car accidents. ___
   (d) The food in the cafeteria is too **stringent,** so we usually pack a lunch. ___

8. (a) The comic gave a good **initiation** of a man getting on a horse. ___
   (b) Justin was **initiated** into the club with a silly ceremony. ___
   (c) The **initiation** took place the first week of school. ___
   (d) The birthday card was **initiated** by all my classmates. ___

9. (a) The house fire **smoldered** for days. ___
   (b) I would **smolder** the larger of the two apples. ___
   (c) A desire for revenge **smoldered** in Mikael. ___
   (d) Rubbing two sticks together caused the dry grass to **smolder,** and we started a fire. ___

10. (a) They found our hiding place, and we ran **headlong** in the other direction, screaming with laughter. ___
    (b) Jeremiah always takes his time to make **headlong** decisions. ___
    (c) I slowly placed the cup **headlong** on the table. ___
    (d) There was a **headlong** rush to buy lottery tickets when the prize reached a hundred million dollars. ___

acrid
casualty
congested
cope
headlong
hurtle
impede
inevitable
initiate
irate
lax
negligent
smolder
stringent
throng

Making Connections

Circle the letter next to each correct answer. There may be more than one correct answer.

1. Which word or words go with *burn?*
   (a) sear   (b) scorch   (c) smolder   (d) stringent

2. Which word or words go with *crowded?*
   (a) negligent   (b) congested   (c) teeming   (d) obnoxious

3. Which word or words go with *angry?*
   (a) exasperated   (b) stringent   (c) lax   (d) irate

4. Which word or words go with *start?*
   (a) impede   (b) commence   (c) launch   (d) initiate

5. Which word or words go with *interfere with?*
   (a) smolder   (b) thwart   (c) impede   (d) initiate

6. Which word or words go with *careless?*
   (a) inevitable   (b) boisterous   (c) negligent   (d) lax

7. Which word or words go with *manage?*
   (a) throng   (b) cope   (c) impede   (d) aspire

8. Which word or words go with *accident?*
   (a) incident   (b) casualty   (c) throng   (d) tower

9. Which word or words go with *bitter?*
   (a) competent   (b) headlong   (c) acrid   (d) lax

10. Which word or words go with *movement?*
    (a) hurtle   (b) hover   (c) motion   (d) negligence

Determining Meanings

Circle the letter next to each answer choice that correctly completes the sentence. There may be more than one correct answer.

1. We are **coping**
   (a) by getting extra help on weekends.
   (b) with the holiday crowds by going shopping in the morning.
   (c) an area thoroughly before deciding to move in.
   (d) people into doing things they know could get them into trouble.

2. **Inevitably**
   (a) I ate more than I should have, just like every year at the holiday supper.
   (b) write your name on the paper.
   (c) sit and think about what you did.
   (d) a healthy heart beats day in and day out.

3. The **acrid**
   (a) smell of burning tires filled the area around the town dump.
   (b) regions of the United States are mostly in the southwest.
   (c) sound of a police siren filled the air.
   (d) taste made the drink hard to swallow.

4. The **casualties**
   (a) spoken by the teacher were written on the board.
   (b) were flown by helicopter to the Westfield hospital.
   (c) from the earthquake are expected to number in the hundreds.
   (d) of love and respect are the best of all.

5. We **hurtled**
   (a) softly underwater in slow-motion.
   (b) through space aboard the rocket.
   (c) with laughter when we heard the joke.
   (d) past home plate to score the winning runs.

6. **Negligence**
   (a) was the cause of the accident.
   (b) can be found on dusty windowsills.
   (c) of a pet is loathsome.
   (d) sounds a lot like humming.

acrid
casualty
congested
cope
headlong
hurtle
impede
inevitable
initiate
irate
lax
negligent
smolder
stringent
throng

7. A **throng** of
   (a) bubbles rose to the surface of the pond.
   (b) colors from red to violet are in the rainbow.
   (c) students gathered outside the pool.
   (d) people lined up at the ticket booth.

8. An **irate**
   (a) parent at the meeting demanded to talk to the principal.
   (b) person is calm and content.
   (c) bear tried to protect her cubs.
   (d) nail scratched my foot.

8D Completing Sentences

Complete the sentences to demonstrate your knowledge of the words in bold.

1. One thing I know to be **inevitable** is

   _____ .

2. When rules become **lax,**

   _____ .

3. A **negligent** driver is likely

   _____ .

4. I **cope** with life's problems by

   _____ .

5. A rule that I think is too **stringent** is

   _____ .

6. If something is an **impediment,** that means it is

   _____ .

7. **Casualties** are produced by

   _____ .

8. When I'm **congested,** I feel

   _____ .

9. I become **irate** when

   _____ .

10. Something that tastes **acrid** is

   _____ .

The Triangle Fire

A hundred years ago, American industry was growing fast and needed workers badly. It found them in the millions of immigrants who poured into the United States from Europe. Most passed through Ellis Island in New York Harbor with little money and few possessions. Many went no farther than New York City in their search for jobs. Young women found employment in the overcrowded, unsanitary, and unsafe factories of the city's garment district. In these sweatshops they worked long hours for low wages. Fire inspections were **lax,** and fire equipment was inadequate. It was **inevitable** that tragedy would strike sooner or later.

On Saturday, March 25, 1911, the top three floors of a ten-story building on New York's Lower East Side were crowded with women working for the Triangle Shirtwaist Company. Late in the afternoon, a bin containing waste fabric on the eighth floor began to **smolder.** No one noticed until it suddenly burst into flames. Women in the crowded workroom tried frantically to put out the rapidly spreading fire, but their efforts were in vain. **Acrid** smoke filled the room. Many of the women, coughing, choking, and unable to see where they were going, were trampled in the **headlong** rush for the only unlocked door in the workroom. The owners of the company always kept the other doors locked to prevent women from slipping outside into the hallway for a break when they were supposed to be working.

Those who fled into the heavily **congested** hallway found that just one elevator was working. Only twelve women were able to use it. The fire escape collapsed under the weight of people crowding onto it. The narrow stairway, less than three feet wide, **impeded** the movement of the women, leaving many trapped. More than forty women jumped from windows and **hurtled** to their deaths eighty-five feet below. Others flung themselves down the elevator shaft in desperate attempts to escape. Firefighters at the scene were unable to **cope** with the situation. Water from their hoses failed to reach the flames because the pressure was too low; their ladders reached only to the sixth floor.

A **throng** estimated at over a hundred thousand people attended the mass funeral of the victims of the fire. Incredible as it sounds, an official inquiry later found that the Triangle Shirtwaist Company had not been guilty of **negligence. Irate** citizens demanded that such a tragedy never be allowed

acrid
casualty
congested
cope
headlong
hurtle
impede
inevitable
initiate
irate
lax
negligent
smolder
stringent
throng

to happen again. As a result of the fire, new safety measures were **initiated.**
Laws dealing with building safety were made more **stringent,** and firefighting
equipment and methods were improved. But the changes came too late for the
unfortunate 145 women who were **casualties** of New York's Triangle fire.

▶ **Answer each of the following questions with a sentence. If a question does
not contain a vocabulary word from the lesson's word list, use one in your
answer. Use each word only once.**

1. Why did the fleeing women have trouble breathing?

_____

_____

2. What happened to the women who jumped from the windows?

_____

_____

3. How many victims were there in the Triangle fire?

_____

_____

4. What is the meaning of **lax** as it is used in the passage?

_____

_____

5. Did anything good result from the Triangle fire?

_____

_____

6. What did the official inquiry fail to do?

_____

_____

7. Why were the citizens of New York **irate?**

_____

_____

8. What is the meaning of **smolder** as it is used in the passage?

_____

_____

9. How did the narrowness of the stairway contribute to the disaster?

_____

_____

10. Did the women leave the work area in an orderly manner?

_____

_____

11. How did their inadequate equipment hamper the firefighters?

_____

_____

12. What is the meaning of **congested** as it is used in the passage?

_____

_____

13. What is the meaning of **initiated** as it is used in the passage?

_____

_____

14. How did the people of New York pay their respects to the dead women?

_____

_____

15. What was so terrible about the lack of fire inspections before the fire?

_____

_____

| acrid |
| casualty |
| congested |
| cope |
| headlong |
| hurtle |
| impede |
| inevitable |
| initiate |
| irate |
| lax |
| negligent |
| smolder |
| stringent |
| throng |

Fun & Fascinating FACTS

- **Initiate** and *begin* are synonyms, but their meanings carry a difference that should be noted. *Begin* is the general, all-purpose word for the start of something; one can *begin* anything, from a sentence to a world war! *Initiate* has a narrower meaning; it suggests taking the first in a series of major steps. (A president may **initiate** a new policy; a teacher may **initiate** new attendance rules.)

  Initiative is the first step in bringing something about. (I took the *initiative* by demanding a change.)

  Initiative is also the ability to get things done without waiting to be told. (You must show *initiative* if you wish to be given the part in the play.)

- **Negligent** means "failing to give proper attention to" and is formed from the verb *neglect*. Another adjective, *negligible,* is formed from this verb; it means "so small or unimportant that it can be neglected or ignored." (The cost of a helmet was *negligible* compared to the price of the bike.)

initiate

verb To begin something; to start a process.

*It's time to **initiate** the rocket for launch.*

....

Word Family
initiation (noun)
initiative (noun)
initiator (noun)

Synonyms and Antonyms
Synonyms: begin, introduce, launch
Antonyms: conclude, finish, wrap up

Discussion & Writing Prompt

Initiative is the energy or ability to start something or take action on your own, without someone telling you what to do. Describe something you take the **initiative** to do at home.

2 min.	3 min.
1. Turn and talk to your partner or group.	**2.** Write 2–4 sentences.
Use this space to take notes or draw your ideas.	Be ready to share what you have written.

Crossword Puzzle Solve the crossword puzzle by studying the clues and filling in the answer boxes. The number after a clue is the lesson the word is from.

Clues Across

1. Expressed honestly and without holding back **(6)**
7. To burn slowly without bursting into flame **(8)**
8. Relating to work requiring little skill **(5)**
9. Short for *Peter*
10. To think about carefully **(7)**
11. A period of rest **(5)**
13. To give freely and generously **(7)**
14. Needing to be attended to at once **(5)**
15. To ask earnestly **(7)**
17. Courage; bravery **(7)**
20. Opposite of *front*
21. To gather or move in large numbers **(8)**
22. Remain
24. To work long and hard **(5)**
25. To stir up interest in a cause **(5)**
26. Failing to pay proper attention to **(8)**

Clues Down

2. Just enough; sufficient **(5)**
3. Very angry **(8)**
4. Amazement or dismay that causes confusion **(7)**
5. Opposite of *rear*
6. Relating to oranges, lemons, and similar fruits **(5)**
9. A special favor given to a person or a group **(7)**
11. Noisy merrymaking **(7)**
12. A first public appearance **(6)**
15. A showing of an unfair preference **(6)**
16. To move with great force and speed **(8)**
18. The Grand _____ is in Arizona.
19. An unpleasant and cramped place to live **(5)**
23. Two sides pull on a rope in a _____ of war.

Study the definitions of the words. Then do the exercises that follow.

dumbfound
dum´ found

v. To make speechless with amazement.
The announcement that my cat Patch had won "best in show" **dumbfounded** me.

dumbfounded *adj.* Speechless with amazement.
The **dumbfounded** tenants stared at the eviction notice in disbelief.

ensue
en sōō´

v. To follow; to come as a result of or at a later time.
When the principal declared the next day a holiday, shouting and clapping **ensued.**

era
er´ ə

n. A particular period in history.
The **era** of space exploration began in the 1950s.

flourish
flʊr´ ish

v. 1. To thrive or prosper.
Plants **flourish** in a greenhouse.

2. To wave in the air.
The softball player **flourished** her hat above her head to acknowledge the crowd's cheers.

n. 1. A sweeping motion.
The star of the show made her first entrance with a **flourish.**

2. A showy burst of music.
The opera begins with a **flourish** of trumpets.

3. A fancy line or curve added to something written.
His artistic nature was expressed in the **flourish** with which he signed his name.

Show your partner how to flourish your book over your head.

garrison
gar´ ə sən

n. 1. Soldiers stationed in a place to protect it.
The **garrison** held off the enemy for four days before capitulating.

2. A military place of protection, together with its soldiers and weapons.
The **garrison** controlled the only passage through the mountain range.

v. To provide soldiers with a place to live.
The commander had to **garrison** the troops in an old schoolhouse.

grievous
grē´ vəs

adj. Causing grief or pain; hard to bear.
It was a **grievous** loss to the entire family when our dog died.

Show your partner how you would look if you suffered a grievous loss.

hoard
hôrd

v. To save and put away, especially secretly.
Squirrels **hoard** acorns for the winter.

n. Anything put away in such a manner.
My **hoard** of comic books includes several authentic 1930s Superman comics.

inundate
in´ ən dāt

v. 1. To cover, as with water from a flood.
The valley was **inundated** when the dam burst.

2. To load with an excessive amount or number of something.
Fans **inundated** radio stations with requests to play the new album.

Tell your partner if you think you are inundated with schoolwork.

invincible
in vin´ sə bəl

adj. Impossible to defeat.
When the Yankees had a fifteen-game winning streak, we began to think they were **invincible.**

With your partner, make a list of superheroes whose powers make them invincible.

nomad
nō´ mad

n. A member of a group that settles briefly in one place and then moves on to another.
The Bedouins of the Sahara and Arabian deserts were **nomads.**

nomadic *adj.* (nō mad´ ik) Having the characteristics of a nomad.
After acquiring horses in the 1760s, the Cheyenne became **nomadic** buffalo hunters on the Great Plains.

placate
plā´ kāt

v. To stop from being angry; to calm.
I was able to **placate** my friend when I explained my reason for being late.

principal
prin´ sə pəl

adj. Most important.
The administration's **principal** objective is to reduce the school dropout rate.

n. 1. A person or thing that is of the greatest importance.
The club owners and the players' agent are the **principals** in the dispute over baseball players' salaries.

2. The head of a school.
The **principal** has the authority to hire extra teachers if student enrollment increases.

3. The sum of money owed, not including the interest.
My parents would need $8,479 to pay off the **principal** on the car loan.

Share with your partner your principal plans for this weekend.

recede
ri sēd´

v. 1. To move back or to drop to a lower level.
The tide **receded** and exposed the rocks near the shore.

2. To become fainter.
The blare of music from the car's radio **receded** as it disappeared into the night.

Talk to your partner about what could make water in a lake recede.

ruthless
rōōth´ ləs

adj. Showing no mercy; pitiless.
Disease and inadequate supplies finally terminated the **ruthless** invader Attila the Hun in fifth-century Europe.

sacrifice
sak´ rə fĭs

n. 1. Something given up for the sake of another.
The parents made many **sacrifices** so that their children could go to college.

2. An offering to a god.
In the Incan culture, **sacrifices** were often made during or after an earthquake, drought, or epidemic.

v. 1. To give up something for another.
I **sacrificed** my privacy by sharing my room with my sister.

2. To offer something of value to a god.
Goats and dogs were **sacrificed** at the ancient Roman festival of Lupercalia.

Tell your partner about a time you sacrificed something to make a friend or a family member happy.

9A Finding Meanings

Choose two phrases to form a sentence that correctly uses a word from Word List 9. Then write the sentence.

1. (a) A flourish is
   (b) a burst of music.
   (c) A garrison is
   (d) a troubling situation.

   _____

   _____

2. (a) A principal is
   (b) an exchange for something else.
   (c) A hoard is
   (d) a collection put away secretly.

   _____

   _____

3. (a) speechless with amazement.   (c) To be inundated is to be
   (b) To be grievous is to be   (d) covered with water.

_____

_____

4. (a) provide them with a place to live. (c) try to satisfy their demands.
   (b) To sacrifice soldiers is to   (d) To garrison soldiers is to

_____

_____

5. (a) a sum of money owed.   (c) Principal is
   (b) a truth by which we govern   (d) A nomad is
       ourselves.

_____

_____

6. (a) calm that person.   (c) To placate someone is to
   (b) To dumbfound someone is to   (d) show that person no mercy.

_____

_____

7. (a) prevented from moving.   (c) speechless with amazement.
   (b) To be dumbfounded is to be   (d) To be invincible is to be

_____

_____

8. (a) An era is   (c) a burst of music that announces
                                               an arrival.
   (b) A sacrifice is   (d) something that is given up for another.

_____

_____

9. (a) lack the means to support   (c) Ruthless people are those who
       themselves.
   (b) keep moving from place to place.   (d) Nomadic people are those who

_____

_____

10. (a) a person of the greatest   (c) A flourish is
        importance.
    (b) An era is   (d) a sweeping motion.

_____

_____

11. (a) A ruthless person is one who   (c) exists only in stories.
    (b) An invincible person is one who   (d) cannot be defeated.

_____

_____

9B Just the Right Word

Replace each phrase in bold with a single word (or form of the word) from the word list.

1. Oil is the **most important** export of Saudi Arabia.

2. John Hancock wrote his name with a **decorative sweeping line** when he signed the Declaration of Independence.

3. In Greek myths, an animal was sometimes **slaughtered as an offering** by a mortal to please the gods.

4. Some people believe you have to be **unwilling to show any pity to those with whom you have dealings** in order to succeed in business.

5. Many childhood memories **gradually become fainter and fainter** as we grow older.

6. The world of art suffered a **serious and very sad** loss when Frida Kahlo died.

7. The **period in history given the name** of the Cold War between the United States and the Soviet Union ended in 1990.

8. If this heavy rain continues, soil erosion will **follow as a result of it.**

9. The **soldiers housed in a protected place** suffered few casualties during the attack.

dumbfound
ensue
era
flourish
garrison
grievous
hoard
inundate
invincible
nomad
placate
principal
recede
ruthless
sacrifice

9C

Applying Meanings

Circle the letter or letters next to each correct answer. There may be more than one correct answer.

1. Which of the following responses might **placate** an irate customer?
   (a) "Don't blame me; I just work here."
   (c) "Would you calm down!"
   (b) "I'll take care of the problem."
   (d) "Let me get the manager."

2. A town can be **inundated** with which of the following?
   (a) floodwaters
   (c) rain
   (b) tourists
   (d) ladybugs

3. Which of the following can **flourish?**
   (a) a business
   (c) a tree
   (b) a country
   (d) an incident

4. Which of the following could be the length of an **era?**
   (a) one year
   (c) a couple of centuries
   (b) twenty seconds
   (d) a couple of hours

5. Which of the following can be **hoarded?**
   (a) health
   (c) food
   (b) wealth
   (d) solitude

6. Which of the following is true of a **nomad?**
   (a) is part of a group
   (c) works at a 9-to-5 job
   (b) has a permanent home
   (d) lives mostly in cities

7. Which of the following applies to the word **principal?**
   (a) It is not a noun.
   (c) It is a noun only.
   (b) It can be a noun or an adjective.
   (d) It is an adjective only.

8. Which of the following can be **grievous?**
   (a) a wound
   (c) a loss
   (b) a respite
   (d) a privilege

9D Word Study: Synonyms

Write a synonym for each of the numbered words. Choose from the boldfaced words below.

consider	joy	amaze	satisfy	hasty
manage	overcrowded	brave	proud	beg

1. cope _____

2. congested _____

3. beseech _____

4. ponder _____

5. gratify _____

6. haughty _____

7. dumbfound _____

8. rapture _____

9. impetuous _____

10. plucky _____

	dumbfound
	ensue
	era
	flourish
	garrison
	grievous
	hoard
	inundate
	invincible
	nomad
	placate
	principal
	recede
	ruthless
	sacrifice

Vocabulary in Context
Read the passage.

The Spanish Conquest of Mexico

For over two hundred years, until it was overthrown by Spanish invaders in 1519, the Aztec empire in Mexico was a prosperous and highly cultivated society. Many arts and sciences **flourished;** the Aztecs developed astronomy, mathematics, engineering, agriculture, sculpture, and music to a far higher degree than did the Europeans of that **era.** At the same time, they were a warlike people, **ruthless** in battle, and their religious beliefs involved acts of extreme cruelty. Prisoners of war were offered as human **sacrifices** to their many gods. The Aztecs believed that the gods had already destroyed the world four times, and unless they were **placated** in this way, they would destroy it again.

The Aztecs were originally a **nomadic** people who lived mainly by hunting. Around the year 1300, they settled on an island on Lake Texcoco. The land there was wet and swampy, but the Aztecs drained the marshes and became farmers. Their **principal** crop was corn; they also grew beans, squash, and chili peppers. Over a two-hundred-year period, they created an empire extending across central Mexico from the Gulf of Mexico to the Pacific. Its capital was Tenochtitlán, which we know today as Mexico City. In 1500, Tenochtitlán was **inundated** by a terrible flood that drowned many of its people. After the floodwaters had **receded,** the Aztecs quickly rebuilt their city, but a far worse catastrophe was to follow.

In 1519, a Spanish explorer named Hernando Cortéz landed in Mexico with an army of six hundred soldiers. He established a **garrison** in what is now the city of Veracruz on Mexico's east coast. His plan was to destroy the Aztec army and take over their country for Spain. Because horses were unknown to the Aztecs, they were **dumbfounded** by the sight of people on horseback. They believed the Spanish soldiers to be gods and therefore **invincible.** Fighting them, the Aztecs thought, would be pointless. So Montezuma, the Aztec emperor, allowed the Spaniards to take over his city without any resistance. Cortéz now gave the orders and Montezuma became a prisoner in his own palace. The Spanish discovered a great **hoard** of gold and silver there. It was later loaded onto Spanish ships and sent to Spain. It is believed that much of the treasure was lost at sea.

When word came that Spanish soldiers had been killed in an attack on Veracruz, the Aztecs realized that they had made a **grievous** error in their previous thinking. These strange creatures were not gods after all! A battle **ensued** in Tenochtitlán, and although Montezuma was killed, the Aztecs drove the Spanish from their city. But their victory was only temporary. Cortéz returned in 1521 with another army that laid siege to Tenochtitlán. After eighty days, the city was forced to surrender. The rule of the Aztecs in Mexico had ended; Spanish rule had begun.

▶ **Answer each of the following questions with a sentence. If a question does not contain a vocabulary word from the lesson's word list, use one in your answer. Use each word only once.**

1. When did the Aztecs give up their **nomadic** way of life?

_____

_____

2. What is the meaning of **flourished** as it is used in the passage?

_____

_____

3. What is the meaning of **principal** as it is used in the passage?

_____

_____

4. Why would thieves have found Montezuma's palace especially appealing?

_____

_____

5. What **grievous** event occurred in Tenochtitlán in 1500?

_____

_____

6. Why would neighboring tribes not want to antagonize the Aztecs?

_____

_____

7. What was an initial part of Cortéz's plan to conquer Mexico?

_____

_____

| dumbfound |
| ensue |
| era |
| flourish |
| garrison |
| grievous |
| hoard |
| inundate |
| invincible |
| nomad |
| placate |
| principal |
| recede |
| ruthless |
| sacrifice |

8. What shocked the Aztecs when they first saw the Spaniards?

_____

_____

9. How do we know that the Aztecs feared their gods?

_____

_____

10. What is the meaning of **sacrifices** as it is used in the passage?

_____

_____

11. Why did the Aztecs capitulate so readily?

_____

_____

12. What **ensued** after the second surrender of Tenochtitlán?

_____

_____

13. In what year did the Aztec **era** end?

_____

_____

14. What is the meaning of **receded** as it is used in the passage?

_____

_____

15. What is the meaning of **inundated** as it is used in the passage?

_____

_____

Fun & Fascinating FACTS

- **Flourish** and *flower* (as verbs) are synonyms; both can mean "to thrive." We can say that the arts *flourished*, or *flowered*, in Athens in the fifth century BCE. Both words come from the Latin *flos*, which means "a flower."

- Don't confuse **hoard**, "something stored away secretly," with *horde*, "a large crowd or swarm." These two words are homophones; they sound the same but have different spellings and meanings.

- Don't confuse **principal** with *principle*, which has three meanings: (1) "a rule or truth by which we govern ourselves" (The *principle* of the separation of church and state traces to the First Amendment.); (2) "a truth from which other truths can be worked out" (One *principle* of plane geometry is that parallel lines never meet.); (3) "a rule or law that explains how something works" (An electric bell works on the *principle* of the continuous making and breaking of an electric current.).

dumbfound
ensue
era
flourish
garrison
grievous
hoard
inundate
invincible
nomad
placate
principal
recede
ruthless
sacrifice

principal

noun A head of a school.

noun The most important person in a company or organization.

adjective Most important.

Academic Context

Offering every student a quality education is the **principal** concern of every school.

A **principal** oversees the teachers and staff of a school.

Discussion & Writing Prompt

What do you think is the **principal** responsibility of a firefighter? What are a few things a firefighter does to carry out his or her **principal** responsibility?

2 min.	**3 min.**
1. Turn and talk to your partner or group.	**2.** Write 2–4 sentences.
Use this space to take notes or draw your ideas.	Be ready to share what you have written.

Study the definitions of the words. Then do the exercises that follow.

aquatic
ə kwät´ ik

adj. 1. Growing or living in or on water.
Water lilies are **aquatic** plants.

2. Done in or upon water.
Swimming is an **aquatic** sport.

assert
ə sûrt´

v. To say firmly; to declare.
Charlie **asserted** that the money entrusted to him was in a safe place.

assertion   *n.* A firm statement or declaration.
No one challenged her **assertion** that Tuckerman's Ravine was too dangerous to hike.

assertive   *adj.* Self-assured; bold and confident.
Because of his **assertive** manner, he was able to obtain an interview for the summer job.

Assert your feelings about a vegetable, such as broccoli.

avert
ə vûrt´

v. 1. To turn away.
I **averted** my eyes from the scary scenes in the movie.

2. To keep from happening.
The driver **averted** an accident by hitting the brake.

Tell your partner what you do to avert being late to school.

bleak
blēk

adj. 1. Without much hope.
The family's future looked **bleak** when both parents lost their jobs.

2. Cold and dreary; exposed to cold winds and bad weather.
Penguins seem to flourish in Antarctica's **bleak** climate.

Discuss with your partner whether the chances for snow tomorrow are bleak or hopeful.

blithe
blīth

adj. 1. Cheerful; carefree.
The children's **blithe** mood is contagious.

2. Not showing proper care; heedless.
The driver showed a **blithe** indifference for the safety of others on the highway.

blithely   *adv.* In a carefree manner.
I knew she was happy when she walked **blithely** out the door.

docile däs´əl	*adj.* Well behaved; easy to handle. Because it was my first attempt at riding, I was given the most **docile** horse in the stable.
dwindle dwin´dəl	*v.* To continue becoming less; to grow smaller in number or amount. My hopes of winning the arm-wrestling match **dwindled** when I saw the size of my opponent's muscles.
lethal lē´thəl	*adj.* Causing, or capable of causing, death. A rattlesnake's bite can be **lethal.**
monitor män´i tər	*v.* To watch closely and frequently; to observe and make note. Some cities **monitor** the amount of pollution in the air. *n.* A video screen used to display information. The librarian checked the **monitor** to see if the book was checked out. *Chat with your partner about how often you monitor the clock during school.*
mutilate myo͞ot´l ăt	*v.* To hurt or damage by cutting into, cutting off, or cutting out. Bakari had to **mutilate** the old book to use it as a base for his diorama.
nimble nim´bəl	*adj.* 1. Able to move quickly and easily. Trinity's **nimble** fingers plucked the harp strings with amazing speed. 2. Showing quickness of thinking; clever. It takes a **nimble** mind to solve such a difficult problem.
plight plīt	*n.* A difficult or dangerous condition or situation. The **plight** of homeless people was the principal subject of tonight's evening news. *Talk with your partner about what can be done to ease the plight of stray dogs.*
ponderous pän´dər əs	*adj.* Heavy and slow moving. The elephant made its way with **ponderous** steps through the water.
verge vʉrj	*n.* An edge, border, or brink. After being on the **verge** of extinction, the bald eagle made a remarkable comeback in the 1980s. *v.* To come close to the edge or border of. The story is not merely silly; it **verges** on the ridiculous. *Share with your partner what you do when you are on the verge of losing your temper.*

| vigilant | adj. Watchful; ready for danger. |
| vij´ ə lənt | Health authorities remain **vigilant** for any signs of the epidemic's return. |

Talk to your partner about things you should be vigilant for as you walk home from school.

10A Using Words in Context

Read the following sentences. If the word in bold is used correctly, write C on the line. If the word is used incorrectly, write I on the line.

1. (a) The grass **verge** by the roadside was a good spot for a picnic. ___
   (b) After the two companies **verged,** they became even better. ___
   (c) The story he told **verged** on being funny without meaning to. ___
   (d) The train **verged** along the track and reached its destination ahead of time. ___

2. (a) An **assertive** person like Asif does not take no for an answer. ___
   (b) Galileo **asserted** that the earth was not the center of the universe. ___
   (c) I challenge your **assertion** that the party will be canceled because of the weather. ___
   (d) I joined the **assertion** because I love reading and talking about books. ___

3. (a) "Don't worry about it," Shondra said **blithely** when I mentioned the money. ___
   (b) The movie takes a **blithe** look at life in the Roaring Twenties. ___
   (c) Chien-Shiung showed a **blithe** disregard for her failing grades. ___
   (d) He **blithely** practiced the high jump every day after school for hours at a time. ___

4. (a) After the fifth day of heavy snow, the number of students who walked to school had **dwindled** to just a few. ___
   (b) Carl was **dwindled** out of bed by his blaring alarm. ___
   (c) The dirt road had **dwindled** to an uneven and overgrown path. ___
   (d) Food was **dwindling** rapidly and needed to be replaced. ___

5. (a) Jericho's **nimble** mind was always coming up with something funny to say. ___
   (b) Grandma's **nimble** fingers went to work repairing the shirt. ___
   (c) Her **nimble** feet stumbled all the time. ___
   (d) Our fingers were so **nimble** from the cold that they lost all feeling. ___

aquatic
assert
avert
bleak
blithe
docile
dwindle
lethal
monitor
mutilate
nimble
plight
ponderous
verge
vigilant

6. (a) My favorite **aquatic** sport is diving. ___
   (b) Seals and other **aquatic** animals bask in the sun. ___
   (c) The spaceship travelled at light speed across deep **aquatic** space. ___
   (d) Kelp is an **aquatic** plant that grows in abundance and has many uses. ___

7. (a) The **plight** of the stranded whales drew worldwide attention. ___
   (b) I couldn't stop thinking about the **plight** of the lost puppy we had found. ___
   (c) We thought we could do something to help his **plight**. ___
   (d) The **plight's** colors were mostly gray. ___

8. (a) The sailor kept a **vigilant** watch for icebergs. ___
   (b) Reporters keep a **vigilant** eye on what goes on in Washington. ___
   (c) The guards had grown slow and **vigilant** and were taken completely by surprise. ___
   (d) **Vigilant** sounds coming from the darkness made us shiver in fear. ___

9. (a) It was impossible to **avert** the disaster that followed. ___
   (b) We **averted** ourselves closer to the water. ___
   (c) I **averted** the unpleasant subject by talking about the weather. ___
   (d) I **averted** my gaze from the accident on the news. ___

10. (a) I recognized the **ponderous** footsteps of Grandpa coming into the house. ___
    (b) Uncle Biyen's **ponderous** jokes are very funny. ___
    (c) The titanosaur was a **ponderous** beast, weighing in at a hundred tons. ___
    (d) A **ponderous** cloud floated high above us, threatening rain. ___

10B Making Connections

Circle the letter next to each correct answer. There may be more than one correct answer.

1. Which word or words go with *happy?*
   (a) ecstatic   (b) bleak   (c) blithe   (d) elated

2. Which word or words go with *skillful?*
   (a) deft   (b) bleak   (c) ponderous   (d) nimble

3. Which word or words go with *watchful?*
   (a) lethal   (b) observant   (c) vigilant   (d) negligent

4. Which word or words go with *causing harm?*
   (a) vigilant   (b) assert   (c) mutilate   (d) scald

5. Which word or words go with *water?*
   (a) drought   (b) aquatic   (c) monitor   (d) lethal

6. Which word or words go with *clumsy?*
   (a) nimble   (b) ungainly   (c) aquatic   (d) ponderous

7. Which word or words go with *watch over?*
   (a) mutilate   (b) monitor   (c) supervise   (d) avert

8. Which word or words go with *death?*
   (a) lethal   (b) slaughter   (c) fatality   (d) aquatic

9. Which word or words go with *well behaved?*
   (a) acrid   (b) docile   (c) obedient   (d) vigilant

10. Which word or words go with *hopeless?*
    (a) inevitable   (b) blithe   (c) bleak   (d) grim

aquatic
assert
avert
bleak
blithe
docile
dwindle
lethal
monitor
mutilate
nimble
plight
ponderous
verge
vigilant

Circle the letter next to each answer choice that correctly completes the sentence. There may be more than one correct answer.

1. A **lethal**
   (a) dose of the poison could be as little as a single drop.
   (b) storm left thirty injured and two dead.
   (c) song came on the radio.
   (d) clue in the crossword puzzle had me scratching my head.

2. We **monitored** the
   (a) number of geese in our yard.
   (b) water quality, looking for a rise in minerals.
   (c) sites most students go to on the Internet.
   (d) popcorn into the microwave.

3. It **verges**
   (a) as fast as it possibly can.
   (b) on the absurd to see the kitten lying with the dog.
   (c) its way across the country in hours.
   (d) on insanity to give this much homework.

4. I **averted**
   (a) an accident by slowing my bike down.
   (b) anything with too much sugar.
   (c) some shoes somewhere in the apartment.
   (d) my thoughts from what had happened.

5. I **asserted**
   (a) the money into twenties, tens, fives, and ones.
   (b) my right to speak freely at school.
   (c) a group of friends together to decide what to do.
   (d) my reasons for voting the way I did.

6. A **bleak**
   (a) review in the local paper put the future of the television show in jeopardy.
   (b) weather forecast caused us to change our plans.
   (c) movie was on last night and filled me with joy and hope.
   (d) climate like Antarctica's is not popular with tourists.

7. A **docile**
   (a) dessert like strawberry shortcake is my favorite.
   (b) cat scratched and bit its owner.
   (c) pet is better for families with small children.
   (d) child can still get angry every so often.

8. **Dwindling**
   (a) food supplies meant we would need to cut our camping trip short.
   (b) temperatures might mean snow is coming.
   (c) his hands together, he stood and made an announcement.
   (d) one thing for another was a fair trade.

10D Completing Sentences

Complete the sentences to demonstrate your knowledge of the words in bold.

aquatic
assert
avert
bleak
blithe
docile
dwindle
lethal
monitor
mutilate
nimble
plight
ponderous
verge
vigilant

1. Something I can **assert** about myself is

   _____ .

2. If a person's fingers are **nimble,** that means

   _____ .

3. A **mutilated** apple looks

   _____ .

4. I'm concerned about the **plight** of

   _____ .

5. A **vigilant** parent would

   _____ .

6. An example of an **aquatic** animal is

   _____ .

7. If you have a **blithe** attitude, that means you

   _____ .

8. A sad book might put me on the **verge** of

   _____ .

9. If a movie is **bleak,** I feel

   _____ .

10. Every day, I **monitor**

   _____ .

Danger: Manatees at Play

The subject of manatees takes us far back in the history of both natural science and imaginative storytelling. Manatees have been in existence for fifty million years. This sea animal was probably what sailors were seeing long ago when they reported visions of mermaids sunning themselves on rocks far in the distance.

Closer observation of the manatee shows it to be a **ponderous** mammal. It measures from eight to twelve feet in length and weighs up to three thousand pounds. The manatee's tapered body, shaped somewhat like that of an overgrown seal or miniature whale, has two front legs and a broad flat tail. The legs and the tail all act as flippers.

Manatees live singly or in small groups. They can eat two hundred pounds of food a day, grazing contentedly on water hyacinths and other **aquatic** plants. A manatee sometimes may stand up straight in the water, often with strings of sea plants hanging like hair from its head.

In the United States, Florida's coastal waters are the manatee's principal habitat. These sea creatures are quite **docile** by nature. In fact, they have no fear of humans; they seem to love company! Manatees allow swimmers to play alongside them, something that is discouraged by game wardens.

Manatees feed just below the surface. They are often unobserved by speeding boaters who may go **blithely** on their way, ignorant of the terrible injuries they have just inflicted. Being struck by a high-speed propeller can be **lethal;** almost a third of all manatee deaths are boat-related. Wildlife wardens estimate that ninety percent of all adult manatees have been **mutilated** by the propellers of speeding boats. The reasons for this are not entirely clear— perhaps the manatees have poor hearing and are unaware of a boat's approach. Perhaps they are simply not **nimble** enough to get out of the way in time.

Because of the enormous increase in the number of powerboats in Florida, for years the manatee population **dwindled,** and the animal's prospects of survival were **bleak.** These creatures were on the **verge** of extinction. But people have become more aware of the **plight** of the manatee. Laws such as the Endangered Species Act and the Marine Mammal Protection Act prohibit harming manatees. More needs to be done, though. People operating powerboats in areas where manatees live need to be more **vigilant.** If they were, many collisions could be **averted.** And speed limits need to be strictly enforced, even though people whose livelihood depends on the boating industry **assert** that too much regulation would cause economic hardship.

Still, something amazing has happened. In recent years, because Florida authorities carefully **monitored** the manatee population and took actions to protect them, an aerial survey showed that more than six thousand manatees now inhabit the area's waters. Manatees were removed from the endangered-species list in 2016.

▶ **Answer each of the following questions with a sentence. If a question does not contain a vocabulary word from the lesson's word list, use one in your answer. Use each word only once.**

1. What manatee behavior could have made sailors mistakenly **assert** that they had seen a mermaid?

_____

_____

2. What kind of plant is a water hyacinth?

_____

_____

3. Is the nature of the manatee similar to that of a predator?

_____

_____

4. Is the manatee population still endangered?

_____

_____

5. Have many manatees been injured as a result of collisions with boats?

_____

_____

6. Can a manatee die as a result of being struck by the propeller of a boat?

_____

_____

| aquatic |
| assert |
| avert |
| bleak |
| blithe |
| docile |
| dwindle |
| lethal |
| monitor |
| mutilate |
| nimble |
| plight |
| ponderous |
| verge |
| vigilant |

7. Why do many boaters go **blithely** on their way after striking a manatee?

_____

_____

8. What could boat owners do to protect the manatee population?

_____

_____

9. What is the meaning of **averted** as it is used in the passage?

_____

_____

10. How do Florida authorities keep track of the manatee population?

_____

_____

11. Why would manatees be described as **ponderous?**

_____

_____

12. What is the meaning of **nimble** as it is used in the passage?

_____

_____

13. Why should we be concerned about the manatee?

_____

_____

14. What is the meaning of **bleak** as it is used in the passage?

_____

_____

15. How do people feel about the manatees' **plight?**

_____

_____

Fun & Fascinating FACTS

- The Latin word for *water* is *aqua* and forms the root of the adjective **aquatic.** Other words formed from this root include nouns such as *aquarium* and *aqueduct,* "a large pipe or channel for water." You might guess that the word *aquiline* comes from the same Latin root. Actually, it comes from a different Latin word altogether, *aquila,* which means "eagle." An *aquiline* nose is one that is curved like an eagle's beak.

- The ancient Greeks believed that the dead went to the underworld, where they bathed in the river Lethe, which caused them to forget their earthly lives. The Latin word *letum,* "death," comes from the name of the river and forms the English adjective **lethal,** "capable of causing death" (a *lethal* weapon).

- The noun **plight** carries with it a reminder of love and marriage in centuries past. Once it was a verb and meant "to promise; to pledge." When two people got engaged to be married, they "plighted their troth." This means they would dishonor themselves if they were not faithful and true to each other. *Troth* is a word that is no longer in use, meaning "loyalty; faithfulness; honor." It still appears as part of the word *betroth,* meaning "to promise to marry."

- Several words come from the Latin *vigilare,* "to be watchful." In addition to **vigilant,** there is *vigil,* a watch kept during normal hours of sleep (Parents keep a *vigil* by the bedside of a very sick child.) and *vigilante,* a person who takes the law into her or his own hands, usually as part of a group.

aquatic
assert
avert
bleak
blithe
docile
dwindle
lethal
monitor
mutilate
nimble
plight
ponderous
verge
vigilant

monitor

verb To watch carefully; to see how a situation changes over time.

noun A video screen used to display information.

Other Meaning

noun A person who watches something to make sure it is safe or fair.

Academic Context

A teacher or aide **monitors** students while they take a test.

Teachers may assign activities to be completed on computer **monitors.**

Hall **monitors** make sure students are where they are supposed to be during class time.

Discussion & Writing Prompt

Describe how doctors **monitor** their patients. What do they do, and why is it important to **monitor** patients closely?

2 min.	3 min.
1. Turn and talk to your partner or group.	2. Write 2–4 sentences.
Use this space to take notes or draw your ideas.	Be ready to share what you have written.

Study the definitions of the words. Then do the exercises that follow.

ballast
bal´ əst

n. Heavy material used to make a ship steady or control the rising and falling of a vessel like a balloon.
The hot-air balloon rose when the water used as **ballast** was released.

buoyant
boi´ ənt

adj. 1. Able to float.
The life jackets are **buoyant** enough to support a 200-pound person.

2. Cheerful and carefree.
The students were in a **buoyant** mood on the last day of school.

buoyancy *n.* The ability to float.
The **buoyancy** of helium balloons causes them to rise rapidly.

Tell your partner about something that makes you feel buoyant.

clamber
klam´ bər

v. To climb awkwardly.
My dad **clambered** onto the roof to get the kite.

detach
dē tach´

v. To separate from.
I **detached** the flower from the bush and gave it to my best friend.

detached *adj.* 1. Not connected.
The house comes with a **detached** garage.

2. Lacking concern; not taking sides.
I tried to stay **detached** from my friends' quarrel.

Detach a piece of paper from a notebook and give it to your partner.

eerie
ir´ ē

adj. Causing uneasiness; strange or mysterious.
The **eerie** sound you heard was just an owl hooting.

fathom
fath´ əm

n. A length of six feet, used in measuring the depth of water.
The wreck of the Spanish ship lay in thirty **fathoms** of water.

v. To figure out; to understand.
We could not **fathom** how the magician made the goldfish disappear.

Tell your partner about something that is true but that you still can't fathom, like how there are more than one hundred billion stars in our galaxy.

pique
pēk

v. To arouse or excite.
Pandora's curiosity was **piqued** by the mysterious box that she was not supposed to open.

n. A feeling of resentment caused by being ignored, insulted, etc.
Ramon did not let his **pique** at being benched for most of the game affect his enthusiasm during the fourth quarter.

Share with your partner your pique about something that happened this week.

probe
prōb

v. 1. To poke or prod.
I **probed** the snow with my ski pole to determine how deep it was.

2. To examine closely.
The *Opportunity* spacecraft, launched in 2003 to **probe** the surface of Mars, was still operating thirteen years later.

n. 1. A long, slender instrument used to examine a wound or part of the body.
The doctor used a **probe** to look for fragments of glass in the wound.

2. A thorough investigation.
The principal's **probe** into the incident led to three students going to detention for a week.

realize
rē´ ə līz

v. 1. To be aware of.
I didn't **realize** how astute you were until you came up with that brilliant idea.

2. To bring into being; to make happen.
I **realized** a lifelong dream by going skydiving.

Talk to your partner about a dream you hope to realize.

rupture
rup´ chər

v. To split or break.
The diggers **ruptured** the water pipe, flooding the basement.

n. 1. A breaking or tearing apart by force.
The earthquake caused a **rupture** in the highway that took three months to repair.

2. The breaking of a friendly relationship.
The **rupture** between Cuba and the United States began in 1961 and was not repaired until 2015.

sphere
sfir

n. 1. An object with all points on its surface equally distant from its center; a ball or globe.
Earth is not quite a **sphere,** because it is flattened at the poles.

2. An area of power, influence, or activity.
The 1823 Monroe Doctrine extended the United States' **sphere** of influence throughout the Americas.

spherical *adj.* Of or relating to the shape of a sphere.
The **spherical** lamp threw light in all directions.

Determine with your partner what is included in the sphere of sports activities in the school.

submerge
sub mʉrj´

v. 1. To go underwater.
From the shore, we could see the dolphins jump and then **submerge.**

2. To put underwater or cover with water.
The tide **submerges** the rocks when it is high.

tedious
tē´ dē əs

adj. Seeming to go on for a long time; boring.
The lecture was so **tedious** that I nearly fell asleep.

tedium *n.* Boredom.
We tried to relieve the **tedium** of our long drive by telling jokes.

Tell your partner about the time of your day that has the most tedium.

ultimate
ul´ tə mət

adj. 1. Final.
Anwar's **ultimate** goal is to be chief of surgery at a hospital.

2. The greatest possible; maximum.
The producer has **ultimate** control over the movie.

n. Something that is the greatest; the maximum.
For his birthday, he received the **ultimate** in video games.

unscathed
un skāthd´

adj. Completely unharmed.
Because of its sturdy construction, the house survived the hurricane **unscathed.**

Choose two phrases to form a sentence that correctly uses a word from Word List 11. Then write the sentence.

1. (a) be baffled by it.
   (b) To realize a dream is to
   (c) make it happen.
   (d) To fathom a dream is to

   _____

   _____

2. (a) material used to make a ship steady.
   (b) a feeling of gloom.
   (c) Buoyancy is
   (d) Ballast is

   _____

   _____

3. (a) A sphere is
   (b) a measurement of depth.
   (c) A fathom is
   (d) something forgotten.

   _____

   _____

4. (a) To probe a person's interest
   (b) is to satisfy it.
   (c) is to arouse it.
   (d) To pique a person's interest

   _____

   _____

5. (a) A sphere is
   (b) A rupture is
   (c) a breaking apart by force.
   (d) an inquiry into the cause of something.

   _____

   _____

6. (a) it is separated from the rest.
   (b) If something is detached,
   (c) If something is eerie,
   (d) it is added to something else.

   _____

   _____

7. (a) a feeling of resentment.
   (b) Pique is
   (c) Buoyancy is
   (d) fear of the unknown.

   _____

   _____

8. (a) is to be unharmed.
   (b) To be tedious
   (c) is to show a lack of interest.
   (d) To be unscathed

   _____

   _____

9. (a) To clamber is to
   (b) remove oneself.

   (c) To probe is to
   (d) examine closely.

   _____

   _____

10. (a) An ultimate task is one that
    (b) is very boring.

    (c) is impossible to do.
    (d) A tedious task is one that

    _____

    _____

11B Just the Right Word

Replace each phrase in bold with a single word (or form of the word) from the word list.

1. The **unnatural and strange** silence that filled the deserted house was suddenly shattered.

2. The police could not **figure out exactly** how the painting had been stolen from the museum.

3. When I moved to Alaska, I didn't **have any idea** how much I would miss my friends.

4. This damaged life jacket may have lost some of its **ability to keep a person afloat.**

5. The principal will head the **thorough inquiry** into the causes of student unrest.

6. I've ridden many roller coasters, but the Corkscrew Cannonball is without a doubt the **one that is greater than all the rest.**

7. While I was telling her my troubles, my friend seemed curiously **uninvolved in what I was saying.**

8. Nuclear submarines can **go underwater** for several weeks.

9. I **climbed with difficulty** over the rocks to get to the beach.

10. A banker by profession, she was also involved in politics, diplomacy, and other **areas of activity.**

| ballast |
| buoyant |
| clamber |
| detach |
| eerie |
| fathom |
| pique |
| probe |
| realize |
| rupture |
| sphere |
| submerge |
| tedious |
| ultimate |
| unscathed |

Applying Meanings

Circle the letter or letters next to each correct answer. There may be more than one correct answer.

1. Which of the following would make a good **ballast?**
   (a) iron bars
   (b) helium gas
   (c) sand
   (d) straw

2. Which of the following could be **fathomed?**
   (a) a purpose
   (b) a puzzle
   (c) a motive
   (d) a mystery

3. For which of the following might a **probe** be used?
   (a) brain surgery
   (b) a soccer game
   (c) a picnic
   (d) a flat tire

4. Which of the following can be **submerged?**
   (a) waves
   (b) the sun
   (c) a submarine
   (d) an anchor

5. Which of the following can be **buoyant?**
   (a) a person's spirits
   (b) a life jacket
   (c) an anchor
   (d) a brick

6. Which of the following might **rupture?**
   (a) a friendship
   (b) a balloon
   (c) a gas tank
   (d) an epidemic

7. Which of the following is **spherical?**
   (a) a pingpong ball
   (b) a hockey puck
   (c) a rainbow
   (d) a globe

8. Which of the following can one **detach?**
   (a) the ink from a pen
   (b) the toothpaste from the tube
   (c) a postage stamp from an envelope
   (d) a page from a notebook

Word Study: Analogies

Complete the analogies by selecting the pair of words whose relationship most resembles the relationship of the pair in capital letters. Circle the letter next to the pair you choose.

1. CIRCLE : SPHERE ::
   - (a) link : chain
   - (b) length : breadth
   - (c) triangle : rectangle
   - (d) square : cube

2. FATHOM : DEPTH ::
   - (a) ocean : water
   - (b) ounce : weight
   - (c) mystery : understanding
   - (d) inch : foot

3. TEDIOUS : EXCITEMENT ::
   - (a) ruthless : mercy
   - (b) irate : anger
   - (c) dumbfounded : surprise
   - (d) warm : heat

4. STRINGS : PLUCK ::
   - (a) clothes : wear
   - (b) drum : beat
   - (c) candle : glow
   - (d) water : flow

5. DELECTABLE : DELICIOUS ::
   - (a) melodious : music
   - (b) dilapidated : building
   - (c) generous : benefactor
   - (d) derogatory : insulting

6. FLOWER : GARLAND ::
   - (a) soil : garden
   - (b) actor : agent
   - (c) seed : plant
   - (d) link : chain

7. FLOAT : BUOYANT ::
   - (a) juggle : nimble
   - (b) sink : aquatic
   - (c) flourish : active
   - (d) probe : eerie

8. HOARD : HORDE ::
   - (a) peek : pique
   - (b) burn : fire
   - (c) lend : bend
   - (d) slice : knife

9. AQUATIC : WATER ::
   - (a) delicate : delicacy
   - (b) solar : sun
   - (c) full : moon
   - (d) spherical : earth

10. SMOLDER : BLAZE ::
    - (a) dampen : submerge
    - (b) clamber : awkward
    - (c) deny : assert
    - (d) avoid : avert

ballast
buoyant
clamber
detach
eerie
fathom
pique
probe
realize
rupture
sphere
submerge
tedious
ultimate
unscathed

Exploring Earth's Last Frontier

By the middle of the twentieth century, the earth's continents had been explored from pole to pole. But even though water covers three-quarters of the earth's surface, much of the deep ocean floor remained a mystery. Auguste Piccard, a Belgian scientist whose curiosity was **piqued** by the unknown, changed that. In 1932, he had broken the world's altitude record by going ten miles up in a balloon. He next planned to design and build a vessel to explore the deepest parts of the ocean.

On October 26, 1948, Piccard made his first dive off the coast of Africa in a bathyscaphe, a large, hollow, **spherical** vessel made of thick steel. The word comes from two Greek words: *bathys*, "deep," and *scaphe*, "a light boat." The bathyscaphe could descend into the inky blackness of the ocean depths. With its powerful searchlights, it could **probe** the ocean floor. Those inside were able to look out through windows made of thick layers of acrylic plastic. **Buoyancy** was provided by huge tanks containing gasoline, which is lighter than seawater. The vessel hung beneath these tanks. Iron weights fixed to the outside of the hull by magnets were used as **ballast,** causing the bathyscaphe to descend.

The first test dive was made in water where the seabed lay just twelve **fathoms** below the surface. Piccard and the other crew member were bolted inside the bathyscaphe, which was then swung over the side of the support ship and **submerged.** As the vessel sank below the surface, it filled with an **eerie** blue light created by sunlight passing through the water. It took just a few minutes for the two pioneers of underwater exploration to reach the ocean floor. Shortly afterward, Piccard **detached** the iron weights; the bathyscaphe rose to the surface.

Several hours passed while the gasoline tanks were emptied; this had to be completed before the two men were able to **clamber** out of their cramped quarters. Despite the **tedious** wait, Piccard was a happy man. His mind was already on his **ultimate** dream, to explore the very deepest part of the ocean. He was asked later if he had been afraid during the descent. He replied that he had total confidence in the design and the construction of the vessel he had invented, and, therefore, he had no reason to be afraid.

Twelve years later, Piccard's son Jacques **realized** his father's dream. He and a United States naval officer descended seven miles in a newer, larger, and stronger bathyscaphe to explore the deepest part of the Pacific Ocean. They knew that if there were a single defect in the metal, the enormous pressure would cause cracks to develop. That would **rupture** the vessel and crush them both. There was no way for them to escape if anything went wrong. Thankfully, the two crew members emerged **unscathed** after their great adventure. Jacques Piccard's father, who at the age of seventy-six was considered too old to make the descent himself, was waiting on the recovery vessel and was the first to greet them.

▶ **Answer each of the following questions with a sentence. If a question does not contain a vocabulary word from the lesson's word list, use one in your answer. Use each word only once.**

1. What is the meaning of **probe** as it is used in the passage?

_____

_____

2. Did the bathyscaphe stay underwater long on its first dive?

_____

_____

3. What caused the first bathyscaphe to sink to the bottom of the sea?

_____

_____

4. Why did Piccard **detach** the iron weights?

_____

_____

5. What strange experience did the men in the first bathyscaphe have as they dived?

_____

_____

6. Why was it necessary to empty the gasoline from the tanks after Auguste Piccard's dive?

_____

_____

| ballast |
| buoyant |
| clamber |
| detach |
| eerie |
| fathom |
| pique |
| probe |
| realize |
| rupture |
| sphere |
| submerge |
| tedious |
| ultimate |
| unscathed |

7. What is the depth of water that is equal to seventy-two feet?

_____

_____

8. How would you describe the period of time between Auguste Piccard's arrival at the surface and his emergence from the vessel?

_____

_____

9. Why was it vital that the hull of Jacques Piccard's vessel have no defects?

_____

_____

10. What is the meaning of **realized** as it is used in the passage?

_____

_____

11. What was the condition of the two men who exited their bathyscaphe after exploring the deepest part of the Pacific Ocean?

_____

_____

12. In what way did Piccard's son Jacques resemble his father?

_____

_____

13. What is the meaning of **ultimate** as it is used in the passage?

_____

_____

14. Why would the bathyscaphe have looked the same from any direction?

_____

_____

15. Why were the large tanks filled with gasoline?

_____

_____

Fun & Fascinating **FACTS**

- The fact that the same word can be used as a unit of measurement and as a synonym for *understand* might at first seem strange. With the word **fathom,** however, the connection is easy to see. Sailors wanting to know the depth of the water would drop a weighted line, marked off in *fathoms,* or six-foot lengths, over the side of the boat. When the weight reached the bottom, the length of line indicated how deep the sea was at that point. Sailors would say that they had *"fathomed"* its depth. By extension, a person who was able to "get to the bottom of" something unknown or puzzling was said to have *fathomed* the mystery.

The word itself has an interesting history; it comes from the Old English *faethm,* the distance from fingertip to fingertip of a tall person's outstretched arms. In many cases, this is about six feet.

- The word **sphere** comes from the Greek word for a ball, which is *sphaira.* By combining *sphere* with the Greek word *hemi* ("half"), we get *hemisphere,* which is *half* of a *sphere.* Earth is divided into a northern *hemisphere* (everywhere north of the equator) and a southern *hemisphere* (everywhere south of the equator). Earth can also be divided into an eastern *hemisphere* and a western *hemisphere.*

ballast
buoyant
clamber
detach
eerie
fathom
pique
probe
realize
rupture
sphere
submerge
tedious
ultimate
unscathed

sphere

noun The shape of a ball or globe.

noun A particular area of knowledge, work, or activity.

Academic Context

In math class, you will learn about the properties of a **sphere.**

Word Parts

Sphere is also a Greek word root meaning "ball" or "sphere." It can be found in words such as *biosphere*. What other words do you know with this root?

Discussion & Writing Prompt

A soccer ball is a **sphere.** What are some other examples of **spheres?** Name a kind of **sphere** that you see or use every day.

2 min.	3 min.
1. Turn and talk to your partner or group.	**2.** Write 2–4 sentences.
Use this space to take notes or draw your ideas.	Be ready to share what you have written.

Study the definitions of the words. Then do the exercises that follow.

abduct
ab dukt´

v. To carry away by force; to kidnap.
Bandits stopped the car and **abducted** the driver.

abduction   *n.* The act or instance of abducting.
According to Greek myth, the **abduction** of Helen was the cause of the Trojan War.

Tell your partner if you think it is possible for people to be abducted by space aliens.

abode
ə bōd´

n. The place where one lives; home.
My summer **abode** was a small cabin that I shared with two other camp counselors.

abyss
ə bis´

n. 1. A deep opening in the earth.
We were afraid to look down as we crossed the **abyss** on a swaying rope bridge.

2. Anything too deep to measure.
The Hubble Space Telescope was built to probe the **abyss** of space.

arbitrate
är´ bi trāt

v. To settle a disagreement between two parties by having a third party make a decision after hearing both sides.
The student council will **arbitrate** the dispute between the French club and the Spanish club.

arbitration   *n.* (ar bi trā´ shən) The act of arbitrating.
We hope the **arbitration** will end the argument between the two friends.

attribute
ə trib´ yo͞ot

v. To think of as coming from or belonging to a particular person or thing.
The song was wrongly **attributed** to the Beatles.

n. (a´ tri byo͞ot) A quality or feature associated with a person or thing.
Wisdom is often considered an **attribute** of old age.

Talk with your partner about how work should be attributed on a group project.

capricious
kə prish´ əs

adj. Likely to change quickly for no obvious reason.
I am always changing from a winter coat to a spring jacket because of our **capricious** weather.

compromise
käm´ prə mīz

v. 1. To settle a disagreement by having each side give up something.
We **compromised** by getting a pizza with peppers on one half for my sister and mushrooms on the other half for me.

2. To expose to the possibility of criticism or shame.
The manager will not **compromise** the restaurant's reputation by serving bad food.

n. A settlement reached by each side giving up something.
The **compromise** required my cousin to work late on Fridays so that she could have Saturdays off.

Discuss with your partner a time when you reached a compromise with a family member or a friend.

devout
də vout´

adj. 1. Very religious.
Devout Muslims try to make at least one visit to the holy city of Mecca.

2. Sincere.
I am a **devout** believer in the goodness of people.

distraught
di strôt´

adj. Deeply disturbed; very troubled.
The children were **distraught** when their pet rabbit died.

enlighten
en līt´ n

v. To inform or instruct; to give knowledge or truth to.
I asked my dad to **enlighten** me as to why he wouldn't let me stay out late.

enlightened *adj.* Free from ignorance or prejudice.
This day-care center takes an **enlightened** approach to early childhood education.

Ask your partner to enlighten you on the meaning of his or her name.

incline
in klīn´

v. 1. To slope or lean.
Instead of being vertical, the post **inclines** slightly to the left.

2. To be likely to; to have a fondness for.
I am **inclined** to talk too much.

3. To bend or bow (the head).
I **inclined** my head so that the barber could trim the back of my neck.

n. (in´ klīn) A sloping surface.
The house lay at the top of a grassy **incline.**

Share with your partner something you are inclined to do after school today.

intervene
in tər vēn´

v. To enter in order to help or settle something.
The playground supervisor **intervened** when the children couldn't agree about whose turn it was.

intervention *n.* (in tər vən´ shən) The act or instance of intervening.
The teacher's timely **intervention** kept the discussion from becoming too heated.

necessity
nə ses´ə tē

n. 1. Anything that cannot be done without or that is greatly needed.
Insect repellent is a **necessity** when camping.

2. The condition of being needed.
I don't see the **necessity** for taking separate cars.

Discuss with your partner something you want to buy soon, even though it is not a necessity.

orbit
ôr´ bit

n. The path taken by an object around a heavenly body such as a star, planet, or moon.
The moon's **orbit** around Earth takes just over twenty-seven days.

v. To put into or be in orbit.
In 1961, the Russian Yuri Gagarin became the first human being to **orbit** Earth.

sacred
sā´ krəd

adj. 1. Holy; having to do with religion.
The Western Wall in Jerusalem is **sacred** to the Jewish people.

2. Worthy of being given the greatest honor or respect.
The engaged couple asserted that they consider marriage vows to be **sacred.**

Tell your partner about a place that is sacred to you, such as a building or a beautiful wilderness area.

12A Using Words in Context

Read the following sentences. If the word in bold is used correctly, write C on the line. If the word is used incorrectly, write I on the line.

1. (a) Nina **inclined** the invitation to the party. ___

   (b) The **incline** led down to the beach. ___

   (c) Some like to be a leader, but I am more **inclined** to be a follower. ___

   (d) Mateo **inclined** his head slightly in agreement. ___

2. (a) The **abyss** is thirty-six thousand feet deep in the Pacific Ocean. ___

   (b) A powerful earthquake can produce an **abyss** that swallows buildings. ___

   (c) Melas Chasma is a nine-kilometer-deep **abyss** on the surface of Mars. ___

   (d) The children dug an **abyss** on the beach and tried to fill it with water. ___

3. (a) When we couldn't reach a **compromise,** we decided not to talk about it anymore. ___

   (b) I **compromised** my sister that I would take her to the circus. ___

   (c) Dalip will not **compromise** his reputation by lying. ___

   (d) Russia **compromises** eleven time zones. ___

4. (a) The bald eagle makes its **abode** near wetlands where fish is plentiful. ___

   (b) The bear rarely ventured far from his forest **abode.** ___

   (c) The reports from Maine **aboded** well for our fishing trip. ___

   (d) The Greeks believed that Mount Olympus was the **abode** of the gods. ___

5. (a) Making sure my room is cool before I go to sleep is a **necessity.** ___

   (b) I don't see the **necessity** of wearing a coat today. ___

   (c) **Necessity** can be found if you swim deep enough. ___

   (d) During the siege, the villagers' greatest **necessity** was drinking water. ___

6. (a) **Devout** members of the church meet daily. ___

   (b) From now on, I plan to **devout** my weeknights to studying. ___

   (c) A few **devout** followers stayed until morning. ___

   (d) We **devout** one hour a day to exercise. ___

7. (a) The mountain is **sacred** to the Ute people. ___

   (b) The knights swore a **sacred** oath to protect the queen. ___

   (c) The food had been left out in the heat and had gone **sacred.** ___

   (d) **Sacred** objects were found in the Great Pyramid. ___

8. (a) A flashlight was all we had to **enlighten** the room. ___

   (b) Marcus Aurelius was one of the more **enlightened** Roman emperors**.** ___

   (c) I agreed to **enlighten** the new student about how our school works. ___

   (d) A visit from Aunt Naaz **enlightened** my day. ___

9. (a) A **distraught** voice called for help. ___

   (b) Marguerite scribbled a **distraught** note that made no sense. ___

   (c) A **distraught** lullaby lulled the baby to sleep. ___

   (d) The women looked **distraught** as they ran into the storm. ___

10. (a) The referee had to keep **intervening** to separate the boxers. ___

    (b) It is important to **intervene** before things get worse. ___

    (c) Parking is banned on **intervening** days during the summer months. ___

    (d) The teacher's **intervention** stopped the classroom from getting out of control. ___

12B Making Connections

Circle the letter next to each correct answer. There may be more than one correct answer.

1. Which word or words go with *universe?*
   (a) solar   (b) orbit   (c) eclipse   (d) abode

2. Which word or words go with *unpredictable?*
   (a) enlightened   (b) sacred   (c) capricious   (d) docile

3. Which word or words go with *kidnap?*
   (a) abode   (b) abyss   (c) abduct   (d) abate

4. Which word or words go with *home?*
   (a) orbit   (b) abode   (c) throng   (d) dwelling

5. Which word or words go with *work out an agreement?*
   (a) negotiate   (b) intervene   (c) arbitrate   (d) compromise

6. Which word or words go with *religion?*
   (a) devout   (b) sanctuary   (c) sacred   (d) orbit

7. Which word or words go with *upset?*
   (a) vain   (b) capricious   (c) docile   (d) distraught

8. Which word or words go with *educate?*
   (a) enlighten   (b) afflict   (c) incline   (d) attribute

9. Which word or words go with *up?*
   (a) incline   (b) exhibit   (c) abyss   (d) sacred

10. Which word or words go with *get involved?*
    (a) abduct   (b) intervene   (c) avert   (d) hurtle

| abduct |
| abode |
| abyss |
| arbitrate |
| attribute |
| capricious |
| compromise · |
| devout |
| distraught |
| enlighten |
| incline |
| intervene |
| necessity |
| orbit |
| sacred |

Circle the letter next to each answer choice that correctly completes the sentence. There may be more than one correct answer.

1. The **orbit** of
   (a) the earth by a human first took place in 1961.
   (b) each of the sun's planets is carefully calculated by astronomers.
   (c) a planet around a distant star has been observed and measured.
   (d) the earth is twenty-five thousand miles at the equator.

2. We **intervened**
   (a) to stop the spread of malaria.
   (b) in the argument when the yelling started.
   (c) the letter before it was sent.
   (d) when the discussion started to get out of hand.

3. We are **compromising**
   (a) that we will eat by six.
   (b) so we can stop fighting.
   (c) our values when we lie.
   (d) by giving each person a little of what they want.

4. The **abduction** of
   (a) Helen by Paris was the act that started the Trojan War.
   (b) electricity was carried along the copper wires.
   (c) dirty water needs to be cleaned immediately.
   (d) someone is a serious crime.

5. The **capriciousness**
   (a) on the book made me want to read it.
   (b) of the wind ended up blowing the sailboat far off course.
   (c) in the old recipe was a secret the chef refused to share.
   (d) of the emperor made his people nervous.

6. To **attribute**
   (a) his poor health to his bad eating habits is probably correct.
   (b) that clearly fake painting to the great Picasso is ridiculous.
   (c) those who served in the military, we have Veterans' Day.
   (d) the team's victory to its fighting spirit seems an accurate observation.

7. The **abyss**

(a) in the price of grapes is due to the good harvest.

(b) known as the Kermadec Trench off New Zealand is thirty-three thousand feet deep.

(c) of deep space appears to have no end.

(d) opened up without warning and swallowed several buildings.

8. **Arbitration**

(a) between warring states is one of the responsibilities of the United Nations.

(b) of dollars into coins was taught at school today.

(c) took place over dinner, and the argument was settled before dessert.

(d) of disputes needs to be done in a friendly way.

12D Completing Sentences

Complete the sentences to demonstrate your knowledge of the words in bold.

abduct
abode
abyss
arbitrate
attribute
capricious
compromise
devout
distraught
enlighten
incline
intervene
necessity
orbit
sacred

1. I am a **devout** believer in

_____ .

2. A **capricious** person

_____ .

3. I could **enlighten** someone about

_____ .

4. Two people need **arbitration** when

_____ .

5. This weekend, I may be **inclined** to

_____ .

6. One **attribute** of a good pet is

_____ .

7. A **necessity** if you are walking in the snow is

_____ .

8. Something I hold **sacred** is

_____ .

9. Something I was once **distraught** about was

_____ .

10. If someone is **abducted,** that means

_____ .

How the Seasons Changed

It is universally acknowledged that the seasons occur because Earth, as it travels in its yearly **orbit** around the sun, has its northern hemisphere tilted away from the sun during northern winters and toward the sun during northern summers. The ancient Greeks were considerably less **enlightened** in matters of astronomy than we are today. They put forward a different explanation. It was expressed in one of their myths about the goddess Demeter and her daughter Persephone.

The ancient Greeks believed that the gods **intervened** frequently in human affairs and often did so in a **capricious** manner. They were **inclined** to regard human mortals as mere playthings. Demeter, whose name means "earth mother," was different. She was a benevolent goddess who had bestowed upon humans the invaluable gift of agriculture, which provided them with most of the **necessities** of life. The ancient Greeks considered the island of Sicily especially **sacred** as they believed it was there that Demeter had first given corn to humans. Women, who tilled the fields and planted the crops while the men hunted, were among her most **devout** followers.

According to the myth, Persephone was **abducted** by Hades, the god of the underworld, while she was in a meadow with her friends picking flowers. Hades suddenly erupted from an **abyss** that he created at her feet and carried Persephone off to his home: the **abode** of the dead. There he made her his wife. **Distraught** over the loss of her daughter, Demeter searched for her everywhere. When at last she determined what had happened, Demeter demanded that Persephone be returned to her. Hades refused. He argued that Persephone had consumed the seeds of a pomegranate while in the underworld. Anyone who had eaten food there was destined to remain.

Unable to agree on a solution to the problem, Demeter and Hades called upon Zeus, the ruler of the gods, to **arbitrate** the dispute. Demeter threatened to make the earth barren unless her daughter was restored to her. Zeus did not want to lose the humans who worshipped him, so he worked out a **compromise.** Persephone would live part of each year in the underworld with Hades. The remainder of the year she would spend in the human world with her mother.

And so, we see, it is to Demeter's moods that the ancient Greeks **attributed** the changing of the seasons. During the summer months, when the land is scorched by the hot southern sun and the crops wither in the heat, Persephone was presumed to be in the underworld with Hades. During the mild, moist months from fall to spring when the earth is fruitful, she was living with her mother.

▶ **Answer each of the following questions with a sentence. If a question does not contain a vocabulary word from the lesson's word list, use one in your answer. Use each word only once.**

1. Were the ancient Greek gods never involved with human affairs?

_____

_____

2. Why was it difficult to predict how the gods might behave?

_____

_____

3. What do we know to be the cause of the change of seasons?

_____

_____

4. What is the meaning of **inclined** as it is used in the passage?

_____

_____

5. Was Demeter indifferent to the loss of her daughter?

_____

_____

6. Did Persephone go willingly with Hades to the underworld?

_____

_____

7. Why was Zeus's **arbitration** of the dispute successful?

_____

_____

8. What is the meaning of **abyss** as it is used in the passage?

_____

_____

| abduct |
| abode |
| abyss |
| arbitrate |
| attribute |
| capricious |
| compromise |
| devout |
| distraught |
| enlighten |
| incline |
| intervene |
| necessity |
| orbit |
| sacred |

9. What is the meaning of **compromise** as it is used in the passage?

_____

_____

10. Why would the Greeks have built many temples on the island of Sicily?

_____

_____

11. Why would the ancient Greeks have worshipped Demeter?

_____

_____

12. Why must the region ruled by Hades have been a very gloomy place?

_____

_____

13. Why do we understand the change of seasons better than the ancient Greeks did?

_____

_____

14. Does Earth go around the sun, or does the sun go around Earth?

_____

_____

15. What are some of the **necessities** of life?

_____

_____

Fun & Fascinating FACTS

- **Abyss** comes from the Greek *bussos,* which means "bottom," combined with the prefix *a-,* which means "without." The adjective formed from it is *abysmal,* which means "too deep or too great to be measured." Because this adjective is often used to modify negative qualities (*abysmal* ignorance, *abysmal* poverty), it has acquired a secondary meaning, "very bad" or "wretched." (The choir's *abysmal* performance was the result of inadequate preparation.)

- The adjective **distraught** is formed from the Latin verb *trahere,* "to draw" or "pull," combined with the prefix *dis-,* "apart." To be *distraught* is to be so agitated or upset that one's attention is likely to be drawn away from or pulled apart from whatever might otherwise engage it. The verb *distract* is formed in the same way. To be *distracted* is to have one's attention drawn away from whatever ought to engage it. (The band playing in the street outside *distracted* me from my studies.) A person who is *distraught* experiences strong emotion; this is not necessarily the case with a person who is *distracted.*

	abduct
	abode
	abyss
	arbitrate
	attribute
	capricious
	compromise
	devout
	distraught
	enlighten
	incline
	intervene
	necessity
	orbit
	sacred

incline

verb 1. To slope or lean.

2. To be likely to do something; to be influenced to do something.

noun A sloping surface.

Academic Context

In science class, you might have learned about simple machines like a lever, a wheel, or an **inclined** plane.

Word Parts

The root *cline* means "lean." The prefix *in-* means "toward." So, **incline** means "lean toward." If the prefix *re-* means "back," what does *recline* mean?

Discussion & Writing Prompt

How do you feel while you run up an **incline?** How do you feel at the top of the **incline?**

2 min.	3 min.
1. Turn and talk to your partner or group.	2. Write 2–4 sentences.
Use this space to take notes or draw your ideas.	Be ready to share what you have written.

Review

Hidden Message In the boxes provided, write the words from Lessons 9 through 12 that are missing in each of the sentences. The number after each sentence is the lesson the word is from. When the exercise is finished, the shaded boxes should spell out a haiku by the Japanese poet Nozawa Boncho. A haiku is a poem of three lines and seventeen syllables, with a subject often taken from nature. This haiku is called "Winter."

1. A thousand-foot-deep _____ blocked our way. **(12)**

2. The _____ of the Roman Empire ended in 410 CE. **(9)**

3. The giant strode with _____ steps across the stage. **(10)**

4. A(n) _____ in the gas line caused the explosion. **(11)**

5. Her _____ attitude cheered up her classmates. **(10)**

6. No serious person would _____ that Earth is flat. **(10)**

7. The Koran is a(n) _____ book to Muslims. **(12)**

8. The _____ of the homeless children broke our hearts. **(10)**

9. I am a(n) _____ believer in the value of exercise. **(12)**

10. A telephone is really a(n) _____ in the modern world. **(12)**

11. Neither side in the dispute was willing to _____. **(12)**

12. Sit down, because what I have to say will _____ you. **(9)**

13. The dog looks fierce but is actually quite _____. **(10)**

14. The spaceship went into _____ around the earth at noon. **(12)**

15. A(n) _____ person will often act on a whim. **(12)**

16. You need to be pretty _____ to play in the outfield. **(10)**

17. I was so _____ by the news that I forgot to call you. **(12)**

18. Minnesota winters can be pretty _____. **(10)**

19. Stuffing envelopes all day is _____ work. **(11)**

20. The ball rolled gently down the _____. **(12)**

21. A(n) _____ sailor happened to see the raft floating by. **(10)**

22. Tell this joke and laughter will _____. **(9)**

23. This machine will _____ your pulse and breathing. **(10)**

24. Count Dracula's _____ was a castle in Transylvania. **(12)**

25. I _____ my success to good luck and hard work. **(12)**

26. These plants will _____ if given plenty of sunshine. **(9)**

27. Your quick action helped _____ an accident. **(10)**

28. Her _____ concern is how to improve her grades. **(9)**

29. We had to _____ over the rocks to get to the beach. **(11)**

30. The _____ prize in the Olympics is a gold medal. **(11)**

31. Listeners _____ KROC radio with their requests. **(9)**

32. Here's a news item that will _____ your interest. **(11)**

33. In 1972, *Pioneer 10* was sent to _____ beyond the solar system. **(11)**

34. By 1945, Hitler's once _____ army was in ruins. **(9)**

35. The machine can _____ your hand if you don't wear thick gloves. **(10)**

36. These ancient and much-feared warriors were _____ in battle. **(9)**

37. The death of my grandfather was a(n) _____ loss to us all. **(9)**

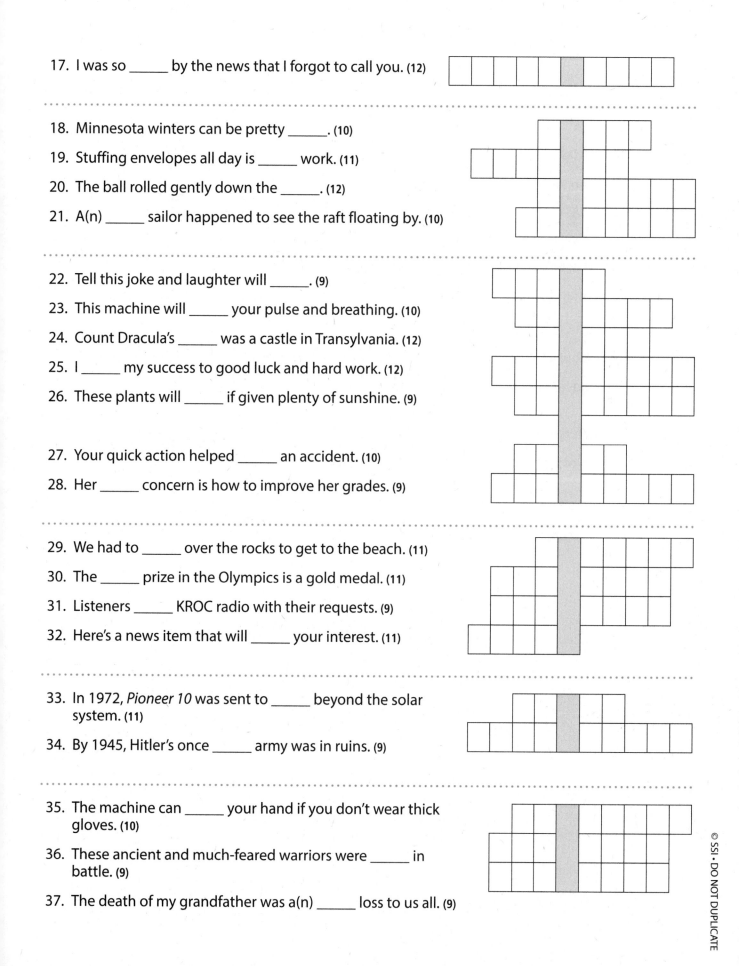

Lessons 9–12 Review continued

38. I cannot _____ his motive for leaving so abruptly. (11)

39. A retired judge has agreed to _____ the dispute. (12)

40. This vessel can _____ and stay underwater for days. (11)

41. At the time, I did not _____ how much I owed you. (11)

42. The kidnappers used a trick to _____ the rare breed of dog. (12)

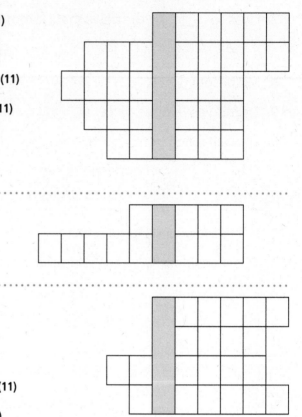

43. Someone who fears hunger may _____ food. (9)

44. A goat was killed as a(n) _____ to the gods. (9)

45. A billiard or pool ball should be a perfect _____. (11)

46. A(n) _____ moves with the herds in search of fresh pastures. (9)

47. Our unexpected victory put us in a(n) _____ mood. (11)

48. We tried to avoid having our energy _____ away. (10)

Study the definitions of the words. Then do the exercises that follow.

arduous är´ jōō əs	*adj.* Requiring much effort; very difficult. Frequent sandstorms made the **arduous** trek across the Sahara Desert even more difficult.
canny kan´ ē	*adj.* Shrewd and careful; watchful of one's own interests. A **canny** student knows what to study for a test.
climax klī´ maks	*n.* The highest point; the greatest moment or event. Roberto Clemente's winning home run in the World Series was a terrific **climax** to the season. *Tell your partner the climax of your favorite book or movie.*
endorse en dôrs´	*v.* 1. To sign the back of a check before cashing or depositing it. The bank teller wouldn't cash my dad's check until he had **endorsed** it. 2. To approve of; to support. Newspapers often **endorse** candidates for public office. 3. To be favorably associated with a product in return for payment. Some well-known athletes are paid millions of dollars to **endorse** products on television. *Ask your partner if he or she endorses the idea of year-round school.*
exuberant eg zōō´ bər ənt	*adj.* Happy and excited; bubbling over with enthusiasm. Our friends gave us an **exuberant** welcome when we arrived. **exuberance** *n.* The quality of being exuberant. The steady rain could not dampen the **exuberance** of fans gathered for the rock festival.
intrepid in trep´ id	*adj.* Feeling or showing no fear; brave; courageous. The **intrepid** astronauts brought their crippled *Apollo 13* spacecraft safely back to Earth.

kindle
kin´dəl

v. 1. To start burning.
A spark from the woodstove **kindled** some oily rags and started the fire.

2. To cause to become excited or stirred up.
The museum's exhibition of Navajo pottery **kindled** my interest in Native American culture.

kindling *n.* (kind´liŋ) Sticks used to start a fire.
There were plenty of dry twigs to provide **kindling** for the campfire.

Share a song with your partner that kindled your interest in learning more about the singer.

lucrative
lōō´krə tiv

adj. Producing wealth or profit.
Our project team believes that a dog-walking service could be a **lucrative** business.

Discuss with your partner your predictions for the most lucrative businesses of the future.

mentor
men´tər

n. A wise and loyal friend and adviser.
As president of the college she founded, Mary McLeod Bethune was a **mentor** to many young African American women.

Talk to your partner about how you could be a mentor for a younger student. What advice would you give the student?

obsession
äb sesh´ən

n. An interest, idea, or feeling that fills one's mind and leaves little room for anything else.
Finishing her second novel has become an **obsession** and leaves her little time for other activities.

personable
pʉr´sən ə bəl

adj. Pleasing in manner and appearance.
The restaurant's **personable** staff made our meal a pleasant one.

proficient
prō fish´ənt

adj. Able to do something very well; skillful.
All the mechanics in this garage are **proficient** in car repairing.

proficiency *n.* The quality of being proficient.
My cousin's **proficiency** in Japanese enabled her to make many friends in Tokyo.

Tell your partner one thing you would like to have proficiency in.

scanty
skan´tē

adj. Not enough or just barely enough; small in size or amount.
After a **scanty** meal of bread and an apple, we continued our journey.

Chat with your partner about what happens to plants that have a scanty amount of water.

strait *n.* A narrow body of water connecting two larger ones.
strāt The **Strait** of Gibraltar connects the Mediterranean Sea and the Atlantic Ocean.

straits *n.* Trouble or need.
When both parents lost their jobs, the family was in desperate **straits.**

zest *n.* Great enjoyment; excitement.
zest Learning to cook meals from many cultures has added **zest** to our dinners.

zestful *adj.* Full of zest.
During the second week of my new exercise program, I awoke each day feeling **zestful** and ready for a five-mile run.

Finding Meanings

Choose two phrases to form a sentence that correctly uses a word from Word List 13. Then write the sentence.

1. (a) A strait is
   (b) a fear without a known cause.
   (c) an idea that takes over one's mind.
   (d) An obsession is

   _____

   _____

2. (a) An exuberant person
   (b) is one who is brave.
   (c) A canny person
   (d) is one who seldom makes mistakes.

   _____

   _____

3. (a) one that is difficult.
   (b) An arduous task is
   (c) A lucrative task is
   (d) one that is done without payment.

   _____

   _____

4. (a) to make it work.
   (b) To kindle something is
   (c) To endorse something is
   (d) to sign the back of it.

   _____

   _____

5. (a) a narrow channel of water.
   (b) A strait is
   (c) a narrow ledge of rock.
   (d) A climax is

   _____

   _____

6. (a) wood used to start a fire.
   (b) Zest is

   (c) Kindling is
   (d) support for a person or a cause.

_____

_____

7. (a) A climax is
   (b) A mentor is

   (c) a person who is vulnerable.
   (d) a wise teacher.

_____

_____

8. (a) keen enjoyment.
   (b) Proficiency is

   (c) Zest is
   (d) the absence of fear.

_____

_____

9. (a) in short supply.
   (b) seriously defective.

   (c) If something is lucrative, it is
   (d) If something is scanty, it is

_____

_____

10. (a) Exuberance is
    (b) Proficiency is

    (c) a state of great need.
    (d) a state of excitement.

_____

_____

arduous
canny
climax
endorse
exuberant
intrepid
kindle
lucrative
mentor
obsession
personable
proficient
scanty
strait
zest

Just the Right Word

Replace each phrase in bold with a single word (or form of the word) from the word list.

1. Getting a telescope **got me excited and stirred up** my interest in astronomy.

2. In this course, students must demonstrate **that they have reached a certain level of skill** in both drawing and painting.

3. Firefighters need to be **unafraid of physical danger** but cannot take foolish risks.

4. This year's citrus crop will be **much smaller than usual** because of the frost damage in Florida.

5. The **greatest event** of the novel was when the knight freed herself from the dungeon and defeated the villain.

6. My mother is a **trusted friend and wise adviser** to several young ballerinas.

7. Mina's part-time baked-goods business turned out to be quite **rewarding in a financial way.**

8. The new television announcer is extremely **pleasing both in manner and appearance.**

9. What **narrow body of water** separates Spain from North Africa?

10. Will the students' parents **give their support to** the controversial proposal?

13C Applying Meanings

Circle the letter or letters next to each correct answer. There may be more than one correct answer.

1. Which of the following might describe someone who is **personable?**
   - (a) ruthless
   - (b) amiable
   - (c) astute
   - (d) haughty

2. Which of the following can reach a **climax?**
   - (a) a game
   - (b) a novel
   - (c) a painting
   - (d) a movie

3. Which of the following could be **endorsed?**
   - (a) a candidate
   - (b) a check
   - (c) athletic equipment
   - (d) a proposal

4. Which of the following can be **kindled?**
   - (a) firewood
   - (b) enthusiasm
   - (c) curiosity
   - (d) negligence

5. Which of the following might be a good **mentor?**
   - (a) an illustrious person
   - (b) a devious person
   - (c) a person devoid of good sense
   - (d) a candid person

6. Which of the following would show a **zest** for learning?
   - (a) reading books
   - (b) asking questions
   - (c) watching cartoons
   - (d) dropping out of school

7. Which of the following can be **exuberant?**
   - (a) a reprimand
   - (b) a welcome
   - (c) a person
   - (d) a compromise

8. Which of the following might become someone's **obsession?**
   - (a) indifference
   - (b) another person
   - (c) food
   - (d) exercise

arduous
canny
climax
endorse
exuberant
intrepid
kindle
lucrative
mentor
obsession
personable
proficient
scanty
strait
zest

13D

Word Study: Synonyms

Synonyms have the same or almost the same meanings, but one often fits a sentence better. Choose the word that best completes each sentence.

arduous / difficult

1. Japanese is a(n) _____ language to learn.

2. The trek across the Gobi Desert was a(n) _____ journey.

religous / devout

3. The Koran is a _____ text that is the basis of Islam.

4. A _____ Muslim prays five times a day.

intrepid / brave

5. The _____ astronauts brought *Apollo 13* safely back to Earth.

6. Josie tries to be _____ when she goes to the dentist.

instruct / enlighten

7. A good teacher seeks to _____ her students.

8. Please _____ the mail carrier to leave any packages for me.

clamber / climb

9. The rosebushes _____ the trellis.

10. I saw the boys run away and _____ up the wall.

final / ultimate

11. Malcolm's go-cart entered the _____ lap.

12. Scientists disagree about the _____ fate of the rain forests.

abode / home

13. Mount Olympus was the Greek gods' _____ .

14. George Washington's _____ was called Mount Vernon.

hopeless / bleak

15. Only penguins can survive the _____ Antarctic winter.

16. Feeling _____ , the candidate dropped out of the race.

stringent/strict

17. Grandma tells us that she had a very _____ upbringing.

18. The product testers performed a series of _____ tests.

surrender/capitulate

19. The police ordered the thief to _____ .

20. The mayor did not _____ to the demand for lower taxes.

13E Vocabulary in Context
Read the passage.

America's First Lady of the Sky

In 1917, Amelia Earhart was working as a nurse's helper in Canada, caring for pilots wounded in the First World War. Their stories **kindled** an interest in flying in the nineteen-year-old girl, so after the war she took lessons and became a **proficient** pilot. As soon as she had saved enough money, she bought her own plane. She soon broke the women's altitude record, taking her tiny biplane up to fourteen thousand feet. By that time, flying had become an **obsession.** Earhart's **zest** for adventure led her to become the first woman to fly solo across the Atlantic. She also became the first person to make the perilous solo flight from Hawaii to California. Previous attempts had claimed the lives of ten pilots.

In 1931, she married publisher George Putnam. A **canny** businessperson, Putnam acted as his wife's manager and was her **mentor** in the ways of business. In addition to being world famous for her exploits in the air, Earhart was **personable** and enjoyed being in the spotlight. This made it easy for Putnam to promote her activities. He published the books she wrote. He got her contracts with advertisers to **endorse** products. He also set up **lucrative** speaking tours in which Earhart talked not only about flying but also about other issues important to her, such as women's rights and world peace. The money they earned in these ways was used to help meet the high costs of buying and maintaining Earhart's aircraft.

On June 1, 1937, at the age of thirty-nine, Earhart took off in a twin-engine Lockheed Electra on a round-the-world flight. Accomplishing this long-term goal was to be the **climax** of her career. The event, which began by

arduous
canny
climax
endorse
exuberant
intrepid
kindle
lucrative
mentor
obsession
personable
proficient
scanty
strait
zest

heading east from California, attracted worldwide interest. **Exuberant** crowds greeted her at every stop of the flight, eager to catch a glimpse of the **intrepid** flier. On the morning of July 2, she took off on the most **arduous** leg of the journey, a 2,500-mile flight from New Guinea to tiny Howland Island in the middle of the Pacific Ocean. Twenty hours into the flight, having covered most of the journey, Earhart radioed that she was running out of fuel. She never made it to Howland Island. Massive air and sea rescue missions produced no clues as to her fate.

Amelia Earhart's disappearance remained a complete mystery for over fifty years. Then, in 1992, searchers found part of a shoe that may have belonged to Earhart, together with some scraps of aluminum, possibly from her plane, on Nikumaroro Island, five hundred miles south of Howland Island. The plane could have crash-landed there when it ran out of fuel. If this is indeed what happened, Earhart and her navigator would have been in desperate **straits.** They could not have survived more than a few days. Temperatures on the island reach 120 degrees. They would have had only a **scanty** supply of water on board, and there was none on the island. Their bodies, and the remains of the plane, would have been swept out to sea in a relatively short time. Is this what actually happened to Amelia Earhart? It is a likely explanation, but we will probably never know for sure. Still, the search continues. In 2015, it was revealed that a piece of aluminum sheeting, measuring nineteen inches by twenty-three inches, found on Nikumaroro Island, almost certainly came from Earhart's plane. Note the word "almost." Nothing has yet been proven.

▶ **Answer each of the following questions with a sentence. If a question does not contain a vocabulary word from the lesson's word list, use one in your answer. Use each word only once.**

1. Why would Earhart have been successful as a television personality?

_____

_____

2. What led Earhart to buy her own plane?

_____

_____

3. How might her flying instructor have rated Earhart?

_____

_____

4. What is the meaning of **endorse** as it is used in the passage?

_____

_____

5. What qualification did George Putnam have to manage Earhart's career?

_____

_____

6. How did the various deals that Putnam set up help Earhart?

_____

_____

7. What two important roles did Putnam play in Earhart's life?

_____

_____

8. What is the meaning of **kindled** as it is used in the passage?

_____

_____

9. Why must Earhart have felt **exuberant** when she flew solo across the Atlantic?

_____

_____

| arduous |
| canny |
| climax |
| endorse |
| exuberant |
| intrepid |
| kindle |
| lucrative |
| mentor |
| obsession |
| personable |
| proficient |
| scanty |
| strait |
| zest |

10. Why was the 1937 round-the-world flight so important to Earhart?

_____

_____

11. Why did the flight from New Guinea to Howland Island require special care?

_____

_____

12. What would have made thirst a particular problem for the stranded fliers?

_____

_____

13. What is the meaning of **straits** as it is used in the passage?

_____

_____

14. What led Earhart to engage in her dangerous exploits?

_____

_____

15. Why would *timid* not be an appropriate word to describe Earhart's flying?

_____

_____

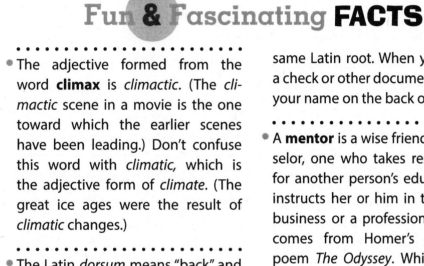

Fun & Fascinating FACTS

- The adjective formed from the word **climax** is *climactic*. (The *climactic* scene in a movie is the one toward which the earlier scenes have been leading.) Don't confuse this word with *climatic,* which is the adjective form of *climate.* (The great ice ages were the result of *climatic* changes.)

- The Latin *dorsum* means "back" and occurs in several English words. The *dorsal* fin of a fish is the one growing from its back; the familiar triangular fin of a shark is perhaps the best-known example. Our vocabulary word **endorse** comes from this same Latin root. When you *endorse* a check or other document, you sign your name on the back of it.

- A **mentor** is a wise friend and counselor, one who takes responsibility for another person's education and instructs her or him in the ways of business or a profession. The word comes from Homer's great epic poem *The Odyssey*. While its main character Odysseus was engaged in his adventurous travels, his friend Mentor was entrusted with the running of his household and with the education of his son Telemachus.

proficient

adjective Good at doing something.

Academic Context

Before receiving a high school diploma, students must be **proficient** in basic reading, writing, and math.

Synonyms and Antonyms

Synonyms: capable, skillful, talented
Antonyms: inexperienced, unable, unskilled

Discussion & Writing Prompt

Think about someone you admire. Is this person **proficient** in a skill or type of work? Explain.

2 min.

1. Turn and talk to your partner or group.

Use this space to take notes or draw your ideas.

3 min.

2. Write 2–4 sentences.

Be ready to share what you have written.

_____

_____

_____

_____

_____

_____

_____

_____

_____

_____

_____

_____

_____

_____

_____

Study the definitions of the words. Then do the exercises that follow.

allege
ə lej´

v. To state as a fact but without offering proof.
I always pack my own lunch, so I don't know why Sari would **allege** that I took hers.

alleged *adj.* Claimed to be true.
The **alleged** theft of my bicycle turned out to be my sister borrowing it without telling me.

allegation *n.* (al ə gā´shən) Something that is alleged.
Our neighbor claimed that my brother was the boy who broke his window, but he could not provide proof to back up his **allegation.**

Allege to your partner something silly that you have no proof of, for example, that your teacher is a spy.

conclusive
kən kloo´siv

adj. Putting an end to doubt; convincing.
The sales receipt was **conclusive** proof that the shirt had been paid for.

Show your partner conclusive proof of your name.

counterpart
koun´tər pärt

n. A person or thing that is similar to another.
The British prime minister is the **counterpart** of the American president.

dismal
diz´məl

adj. 1. Dark or extremely gloomy.
The **dismal** weather kept us inside for most of our summer vacation.

2. Causing misery or sadness; depressing.
The **dismal** conditions in Haiti forced many to flee their homeland.

Discuss with your partner something that would make the weekend dismal instead of fun.

enthrall
en thrôl´

v. To hold the attention of as though under a spell.
The acrobats on the trapeze **enthralled** the circus audience.

enthralling *adj.* Having the power to enthrall.
The children listened for over an hour to the storyteller's **enthralling** tales.

exotic
eg zät´ik

adj. Fascinating because of being very different from the ordinary.
Rare orchids and other **exotic** flowers decorated the tables at the wedding.

incredulous
in krej´ ə ləs

adj. 1. Doubtful; skeptical.
The teacher was **incredulous** when the student claimed to have read the novel in two hours.

2. Showing disbelief.
My friend gave me an **incredulous** look when I said I had seen a flying saucer.

incredulity *n.* (in krə dyoo´ lə tē) Doubt or disbelief.
My father gave me a look of **incredulity** when I said I had asked for extra homework.

Tell your partner something an incredulous person might say.

legendary
lej´ ən der ē

adj. 1. Well known; famous and much talked about over a long period of time.
Harriet Tubman, who led more than three hundred enslaved people to freedom, is a **legendary** figure in American history.

2. Relating to a story (usually untrue) handed down from the past.
Paul Bunyan, the **legendary** lumberjack of fantastic size and strength, is the hero of many "tall tales."

lurk
lʊrk

v. To prowl or lie hidden, as though about to attack.
The farmer frightened away the fox that **lurked** by the henhouse.

Chat with your partner where a house cat might lurk and why.

menagerie
mə naj´ ər ē

n. A collection of animals kept in cages for showing to the public.
The owner of the **menagerie** assured us that the animals were well cared for.

naive
nä ēv´

adj. 1. Inexperienced; ready to accept without analyzing.
I was **naive** to believe that sending off the coupon would win me a free vacation in Hawaii.

2. Simple in a childlike way; innocent.
Even though he is nine years old, he maintains a **naive** belief in the tooth fairy.

Share with your partner one way you were naive in your expectations about seventh grade.

pander
pan´ dər

v. To give or promise what is wanted in order to please someone.
I believe that she **panders** to students by giving them better grades than they deserve.

plausible
plô´ zə bəl

adj. Seeming to be true but not necessarily so.
Lin Shao's explanation of why she was late seems **plausible,** so I'll accept it.

Rehearse with your partner some plausible excuses for not finishing your homework.

preposterous prē päs´ tər əs	*adj.* Too absurd to be believed; ridiculous. You cannot believe this **preposterous** newspaper story that a six-month-old baby speaks three languages.
scrupulous skrōō´ pyə ləs	*adj.* 1. Marked by close attention to the smallest detail. Daniela kept a **scrupulous** record of all her homework assignments. 2. Acting in a correct and honest manner. The children were **scrupulous** in the way they divided the money from the lemonade stand.

14A Using Words in Context

Read the following sentences. If the word in bold is used correctly, write C on the line. If the word is used incorrectly, write I on the line.

1. (a) Grab the milk off the **counterpart.** ___
   (b) The star player has no **counterpart** in any other soccer league. ___
   (c) I use a comb to create the **counterpart** in my hair. ___
   (d) One twin's **counterpart** is the other twin. ___

2. (a) The **legendary** pirate Blackbeard is the subject of several stories. ___
   (b) Grandpa's memory got increasingly **legendary** as he got older. ___
   (c) The eight-year-old violinist's talent was **legendary.** ___
   (d) Lisa was **legendary** in the frigid temperatures. ___

3. (a) My teacher had an **enthralling** tale to tell of his visit to China. ___
   (b) Backstage, we were **enthralled** by the star's presence. ___
   (c) The animals were **enthralled** within a wooden fence. ___
   (d) The **enthralled** people demanded their freedom. ___

4. (a) His **preposterous** outfit included sandals and a tuxedo. ___
   (b) The grass is **preposterous** and green. ___
   (c) His claim that he can see the future is **preposterous.** ___
   (d) How can you tell which mushrooms are **preposterous** and which are safe to eat? ___

5. (a) The challenger has **alleged** ahead of her opponent in the game. ___
   (b) The **allegation** was made that Kiki cheated on her quiz. ___
   (c) The article **alleges** that the library is running out of money. ___
   (d) The **allegation** of a dog can be done in a tub or shower. ___

6. (a) I was **incredulous** when the famous novelist said she wanted to meet me. ___
   (b) Zariah's story was so **incredulous** that nobody took it seriously. ___
   (c) The story that he had found a long-lost treasure was greeted with **incredulity.** ___
   (d) My **incredulity** increased as more absurd details came out. ___

7. (a) The cast members were naturally upset by the **dismal** reviews. ___
   (b) The **dismal** weather ruined our vacation. ___
   (c) Plants become **dismal** if they get too much sun. ___
   (d) The **dismal** sound of the foghorn carried for miles across the ocean. ___

8. (a) The teenager is not a **plausible** candidate for president. ___
   (b) Jerome's story is certainly **plausible,** but is it true? ___
   (c) Make sure your excuse is **plausible** if you want it to be believed. ___
   (d) Astronomers believe that a **plausible** planet is out there waiting to be discovered. ___

9. (a) A **scrupulous** inspection of the train is carried out twice a year. ___
   (b) DeShawn paid **scrupulous** attention to every detail of the feast he prepared for us. ___
   (c) Rafi is **scrupulous** about saving his money. ___
   (d) The **scrupulous** light from the moon covered the street. ___

10. (a) I was **naive** to think that I would get to go on the trip. ___
    (b) The soldiers made several **naive** attacks and won. ___
    (c) The young child's **naive** answers were cute. ___
    (d) The bride wore a dress of **naive** silk trimmed with pearls. ___

allege
conclusive
counterpart
dismal
enthrall
exotic
incredulous
legendary
lurk
menagerie
naive
pander
plausible
preposterous
scrupulous

14B

Making Connections

Circle the letter next to each correct answer. There may be more than one correct answer.

1. Which word or words go with *fascinating?*
   - (a) awesome
   - (b) exotic
   - (c) enthralling
   - (d) incredulous

2. Which word or words go with *give in to?*
   - (a) enlighten
   - (b) lurk
   - (c) allege
   - (d) pander

3. Which word or words go with *no doubt?*
   - (a) conclusive
   - (b) exotic
   - (c) naive
   - (d) plausible

4. Which word or words go with *animals?*
   - (a) menagerie
   - (b) pander
   - (c) domesticated
   - (d) impunity

5. Which word or words go with *danger?*
   - (a) counterpart
   - (b) lurk
   - (c) peril
   - (d) jeopardy

6. Which word or words go with *silly?*
   - (a) absurd
   - (b) ridiculous
   - (c) preposterous
   - (d) scrupulous

7. Which word or words go with *strict?*
   - (a) plausible
   - (b) exotic
   - (c) scrupulous
   - (d) stringent

8. Which word or words go with *believable?*
   - (a) incredulous
   - (b) plausible
   - (c) preposterous
   - (d) scrupulous

9. Which word or words go with *claim?*
   - (a) enthrall
   - (b) allege
   - (c) pander
   - (d) soothe

10. Which word or words go with *sad?*
    - (a) melancholy
    - (b) dismal
    - (c) bleak
    - (d) scrupulous

Circle the letter next to each answer choice that correctly completes the sentence. There may be more than one correct answer.

1. An **exotic**
   (a) fruit like the kiwi is very popular.
   (b) flower grew in the jungle.
   (c) book always has an enormous number of pages.
   (d) destination might be the Caribbean islands.

2. **Incredulity**
   (a) was on their faces when I told them I won the contest.
   (b) showed up in the walls after the heavy rain.
   (c) was removed from the fruit.
   (d) became belief once I realized she was telling the truth.

3. **Conclusive**
   (a) pencils rolled off the desk.
   (b) research shows no link between hair color and intelligence.
   (c) reports said the fire was under control.
   (d) dimes and quarters are in my pocket.

4. **Enthralling**
   (a) people without giving them a chance isn't fair.
   (b) children was the professional clown's favorite thing to do.
   (c) performances by the actors made the school play a success.
   (d) memories remind me just how awesome the trip was.

5. **Lurking**
   (a) at the back of his mind was his fear of failing.
   (b) for catfish is a local tradition.
   (c) in a hammock is my idea of relaxing.
   (d) in the gloom, the coyote got ready to spring at its prey.

6. The **menagerie**
   (a) had animal exhibits that were open to the public every day of the year.
   (b) of choices made it hard for me to decide.
   (c) is privately owned and features a pair of chimpanzees.
   (d) was published in Italy and is five hundred years old.

| allege |
| conclusive |
| counterpart |
| dismal |
| enthrall |
| exotic |
| incredulous |
| legendary |
| lurk |
| menagerie |
| naive |
| pander |
| plausible |
| preposterous |
| scrupulous |

7. I was **naive**
    (a) in French, but I tried to learn anyway.
    (b) for one day a week until I was fourteen.
    (c) to believe that wishing for something always makes it happen.
    (d) when I was young, but I'm a lot smarter now.

8. **Pandering**
    (a) to people's prejudices is wrong.
    (b) to people by promising money never works.
    (c) alligators by feeding them is dangerous.
    (d) off the subject made me forget what I was going to say.

14D   Completing Sentences

Complete the sentences to demonstrate your knowledge of the words in bold.

1. One **legendary** figure from the past is

    _____ .

2. You are being **naive** if you believe that

    _____ .

3. It's **plausible** to think that

    _____ .

4. It would be **enthralling** to

    _____ .

5. To support an **allegation,** you need

    _____ .

6. I was recently in a **dismal** mood because

    _____ .

7. Something I find **preposterous** is

    _____ .

8. Doctors need to be **scrupulous** about

    _____ .

9. In a **menagerie,** you might find

    _____ .

10. I would be **incredulous** if

    _____ .

Bigfoot: Fact or Fantasy?

When European explorers returned from Asia and Africa in the Middle Ages, they reported having seen twelve-foot lizards with huge jaws that could eat a person whole. Most people who heard these stories were **incredulous** and accused the travelers of lying. The stories seemed **preposterous** to them. At that time hardly anyone in Europe had ever seen a crocodile. For centuries, travelers have been ridiculed for their reports of **exotic** creatures seen in distant lands. But the Komodo dragon of Indonesia, the giant panda of Western China, and the mountain gorilla of Ethiopia, to mention just three that were dismissed at one time as imaginary, really do exist.

More recently, there have been stories of Bigfoot, the **legendary** ape-like creature of the American Northwest. And Bigfoot's **counterpart** is said to live just below the snowline in the Himalayan Mountains of Asia. It is the yeti, also known as the Abominable Snowman. **Alleged** sightings, and even photographs, of both creatures make news periodically. Plaster casts have supposedly been made of their footprints. But the photographs are never sharp, the plaster casts could well be fakes, and the claims of those who say they have seen Bigfoot are not very **plausible.** Scientists have been **scrupulous** in their examination of the evidence. Their view is that it is not **conclusive.** Most remain unconvinced that Bigfoot and the yeti actually exist.

In spite of the scientists' findings, some people feel the need to believe that such creatures do exist. Such people are **enthralled** by the mysterious. They would like to think that somewhere deep in the forest, Bigfoot is **lurking.** They imagine that high in the Himalayas, a team of mountaineers is about to come upon the yeti. Supermarket tabloids **pander** to these people. They print headlines such as "Bigfoot Stole My Baby" or "Yeti Attacks Climbers on Mount Everest." Of course, only the most **naive** people believe such stories.

Given our **dismal** record of dealing with wild creatures, it would probably be best for Bigfoot and the yeti, if indeed they *are* real, to remain undiscovered. What would we do with them if we captured them? Such creatures do not belong in a **menagerie** to be peered at and photographed by sightseers. Such is the fate of the giant panda, the Komodo dragon, and the mountain gorilla. Bigfoot and the yeti are probably best left where they are now, creatures of our imagination, along with unicorns, fire-breathing dragons, and mermaids.

allege
conclusive
counterpart
dismal
enthrall
exotic
incredulous
legendary
lurk
menagerie
naive
pander
plausible
preposterous
scrupulous

► **Answer each of the following questions with a sentence. If a question does not contain a vocabulary word from the lesson's word list, use one in your answer. Use each word only once.**

1. Do tabloid newspapers do a responsible job of reporting the news?

   _____

   _____

2. What is the meaning of **naive** as it is used in the passage?

   _____

   _____

3. What do Bigfoot and the Abominable Snowman have in common?

   _____

   _____

4. How does the yeti compare with Bigfoot?

   _____

   _____

5. What do many people imagine Bigfoot to be doing?

   _____

   _____

6. Where does the passage say a creature like Bigfoot would *not* belong?

   _____

   _____

7. What is the meaning of **incredulous** as it is used in the passage?

   _____

   _____

8. What is the meaning of **scrupulous** as it is used in the passage?

   _____

   _____

9. Why does the passage describe spottings of Bigfoot as "**alleged**"?

   _____

   _____

10. Why do most people not accept claims of Bigfoot sightings?

_____

_____

11. What kind of evidence would lead scientists to believe that Bigfoot exists?

_____

_____

12. What would be a likely reaction of people, should there be a more convincing account of a Bigfoot sighting?

_____

_____

13. What is the meaning of **dismal** as it is used in the passage?

_____

_____

14. Why would a rabbit not be considered an **exotic** creature?

_____

_____

15. Why would a report that a unicorn had been spotted be **preposterous?**

_____

_____

| allege |
| conclusive |
| counterpart |
| dismal |
| enthrall |
| exotic |
| incredulous |
| legendary |
| lurk |
| menagerie |
| naive |
| pander |
| plausible |
| preposterous |
| scrupulous |

Fun & Fascinating FACTS

- The adjective **dismal** is formed from two Latin words: *dies,* "day," and *mal,* "bad." It is easy to see how having a bad day might make a person feel *dismal.*

- The Old English word *thrael* means "a slave" and survives in our modern English word **enthrall,** one of whose meanings is "to enslave." The more common meaning, "to hold as if in a spell," can suggest a kind of enslavement; to be *enthralled* by someone is to be so fascinated by him or her that one surrenders one's will to that person.

- The Latin verb *credere* means "to believe" and is used in the formation of a number of English words. *Credulous* persons are easily fooled because they are inclined to believe whatever they are told, no matter how unlikely. On the other hand, persons who are **incredulous** find it hard to believe what they are being told. A *credible* story is one that sounds believable. An *incredible* story is one that is hard to believe.

- A *scruple* is a twinge or sense of guilt felt when one wants to do something that one shouldn't. A **scrupulous** person is someone who has scruples and won't do something that is wrong or dishonest. Some people have no scruples and will do whatever is necessary to further their own purposes. They are *unscrupulous.*

conclusive

adjective Proving that something is definitely true.

*My mother wanted **conclusive** proof that my dog ate my homework.*

Word Family
conclusively (adverb)
conclusiveness (noun)
in**conclusive** (adjective)
in**conclusive**ly (adverb)

Synonyms and Antonyms
Synonyms: absolute, clear, convincing, unquestionable
Antonyms: doubtful, questionable, unclear

Discussion & Writing Prompt

You have found out that a giant eagle is living on your roof. Describe what **conclusive** evidence might prove you're telling the truth.

2 min.	3 min.
1. Turn and talk to your partner or group.	**2.** Write 2–4 sentences.
Use this space to take notes or draw your ideas.	Be ready to share what you have written.

Study the definitions of the words. Then do the exercises that follow.

complement
käm´ plə mənt

n. 1. Something that completes or makes perfect.
Candles will be the perfect **complement** for an elegant dinner.

2. The number or amount that makes up a whole.
The shelf has a full **complement** of books.

v. To bring to completion or perfection.
These traditional Mexican folk songs will **complement** my collection of music from around the world.

Tell your partner what side dish you think is the best complement for pasta.

component
kəm pō´ nənt

n. Any of the more important parts of a whole.
The circuit board is the main **component** of a cell phone.

adj. Contributing to form a whole.
Hydrogen and oxygen are **component** parts of a water molecule.

Chat with your partner about what you think is the most important component of a salad.

conjure
kän´ jər

v. 1. To call forth by magic, or as if by magic.
My interesting cousin claims that he can **conjure** spirits.

2. (with *up*) To bring to mind; to recall or evoke.
The aroma of baking bread **conjures** up memories of my childhood.

emphasize
em´ fə sīz

v. To give special attention to; to stress.
The teacher **emphasized** that homework must be turned in on time.

emphasis *n.* (em´ fə sis) Special attention directed at something to give it importance.
The course puts a special **emphasis** on the causes of the Civil War.

emphatic *adj.* (em fat´ ik) Said or done with force.
Because of my sister's allergies, my parents were **emphatic** that we would never have a dog.

Talk to your partner with emphasis about the weather today.

homage
häm´ ij

n. Honor or respect shown publicly.
On Veterans Day, we pay **homage** to those who served their country.

impromptu
im prämp´ tōō

adj. Unplanned.
She gave a charming **impromptu** speech when called upon by the host.

adv. Without preparation.
This speech course teaches students to speak **impromptu.**

With your partner, come up with one idea for an impromptu party.

lush
lush

adj. Marked by richness of growth, especially of vegetation.
Arid volcanic terrain contrasts sharply with **lush** mountains on the island's opposite side.

medley
med´ lē

n. 1. A mixture of often unrelated things.
On the yard sale's bargain table was a **medley** of objects priced at under a dollar.

2. A selection of music from various sources, played as one piece.
The concert ended with a **medley** of patriotic tunes.

oblige
ə blīj´

v. 1. To require someone to do something for legal, social, or moral reasons.
Joining the book club **obliges** you to buy four selections over the year.

2. To earn the gratitude of.
You will **oblige** me by saying no more about this matter.

3. To do a favor for.
We begged the singer to **oblige** us with one final song.

Discuss with your partner whether students should be obliged to dress in uniform for school.

pretentious
prē ten´ shəs

adj. Drawing undeserved or inappropriate attention to oneself; showy.
Was it **pretentious** of John Hancock to sign his name so conspicuously to the Declaration of Independence?

Tell your partner about a book or movie character who speaks in a pretentious way.

prowess
prou´ əs

n. Great skill or ability.
The political **prowess** of President Franklin D. Roosevelt made him an outstanding world leader.

rustic
rus´ tik

adj. 1. Of or relating to country life or people.
The pictures of grazing cows gave a certain **rustic** charm to the room.

2. Lacking elegance or polish.
A **rustic** cabin of rough-hewn logs was our home for the summer.

n. A country person, especially one thought of as simple or crude.
Shakespeare's **rustics** provide much of the humor in his comedies.

subtle
sut´l

adj. 1. So slight as to be not easily seen or understood.
Jeff's **subtle** hints that he wanted a skateboard for his birthday went unnoticed by his parents.

2. Able to understand fine shades of meaning.
Carolina's **subtle** mind immediately saw a way to make the plan work.

subtlety *n.* Something so slight that only a clever or well-educated person can see it; the quality of being subtle.
The professor pointed out the **subtlety** of the poet's message in her later works.

Using words or facial expressions, give your partner a subtle clue about your mood today.

vocation
vō kā´ shən

n. A person's employment; occupation.
Carpentry started out as a hobby but soon became my grandmother's **vocation.**

vocational *adj.* Having to do with a person's career.
I plan to study physical therapy at the county **vocational** school.

warble
wôr´ bəl

v. To sing in a melodious manner.
Somewhere in the gathering darkness, a nightingale began to **warble.**

15A Finding Meanings

Choose two phrases to form a sentence that correctly uses a word from Word List 15. Then write the sentence.

1. (a) To emphasize something is to
   (b) To warble something is to
   (c) deny it ever happened.
   (d) stress its importance.

   _____

   _____

2. (a) A subtle element is
   (b) A component element is
   (c) one that contributes to making up a whole.
   (d) one that can be easily replaced.

   _____

   _____

3. (a) sing it.
   (b) praise it.
   (c) To complement something is to
   (d) To warble something is to

   _____

   _____

4. (a) a state of doubt or uncertainty. (c) Homage is
   (b) Prowess is   (d) honor paid in public.

   _____

   _____

5. (a) deals with career planning. (c) A pretentious guide
   (b) A vocational guide   (d) deals with low-cost travel.

   _____

   _____

6. (a) that draws undue attention   (c) A rustic sign is one
       to itself.
   (b) that is in need of repair.   (d) A pretentious sign is one

   _____

   _____

7. (a) make light of it.   (c) To complement something is to
   (b) bring it to completion.   (d) To conjure up something is to

   _____

   _____

8. (a) A lush garden is one   (c) that is open to the public.
   (b) A rustic garden is one   (d) with a rich growth of vegetation.

   _____

   _____

| complement |
| component |
| conjure |
| emphasize |
| homage |
| impromptu |
| lush |
| medley |
| oblige |
| pretentious |
| prowess |
| rustic |
| subtle |
| vocation |
| warble |

9. (a) to do that person a favor.   (c) To conjure up someone is
   (b) make that person disappear.   (d) To oblige someone is

   _____

   _____

10. (a) An impromptu change   (c) is one that is very slight.
    (b) A subtle change   (d) is one that is unavoidable.

   _____

   _____

1. Edith Wharton's novels are noted for their **fine qualities that may not be immediately obvious to the casual reader.**

2. This lace tablecloth is a perfect **finishing touch** to your fine china and silverware.

3. Pelé's **great skill** with a soccer ball made him a legendary figure.

4. Although he may look like a **simple country person,** my neighbor is a very astute businessperson.

5. Your mention of lobsters **makes me think back and brings** up memories of that summer we spent in Maine.

6. In both our beginners' and advanced scuba-diving courses, the **most important lesson that is taught** is on safety.

7. If you are cast as the lead role in the play, you are **left with no choice and will be forced** to come to all the rehearsals.

8. The orchestra opened the concert with a **wide-ranging selection** of Broadway show tunes.

9. Politicians must be able to speak **without any preparation and without notes** on just about any subject.

10. Gardening was both her **chosen profession** and her hobby.

15c

Applying Meanings

Circle the letter or letters next to each correct answer. There may be more than one correct answer.

1. Which of the following might be a **vocation?**
   (a) teaching
   (b) nursing
   (c) napping
   (d) flying

2. What might a farm have a full **complement** of?
   (a) computers
   (b) tractors
   (c) clouds
   (d) animals

3. Which of the following can be **conjured** up?
   (a) a fond memory
   (b) a piece of music
   (c) a past event
   (d) a line of poetry

4. To which of the following might we pay **homage?**
   (a) an intrepid war hero
   (b) a great writer
   (c) an illustrious film actor
   (d) a former president

5. Which of the following is a **rustic** scene?
   (a) a Vermont covered bridge
   (b) a Florida citrus grove
   (c) a New Hampshire lake
   (d) a New York skyscraper

6. Which of the following might be **subtle?**
   (a) a suggestion
   (b) a line of poetry
   (c) a shift of mood
   (d) a circus clown

7. Which of the following might **oblige** a person?
   (a) making a promise
   (b) accepting an offer
   (c) borrowing money
   (d) repaying a loan

8. Which of the following might be **lush?**
   (a) a meadow
   (b) a tropical rain forest
   (c) a valley
   (d) a desert

complement
component
conjure
emphasize
homage
impromptu
lush
medley
oblige
pretentious
prowess
rustic
subtle
vocation
warble

15D

Word Study: Analogies

Complete the analogies by selecting the pair of words whose relationship most resembles the relationship of the pair in capital letters. Circle the letter next to the pair you choose.

1. SKILL : PROWESS ::
   (a) consternation : fear
   (b) fire : smoke
   (c) orbit : planet
   (d) journey : destination

2. WARBLE : SONG ::
   (a) applaud : discovery
   (b) receive : gift
   (c) invite : audience
   (d) recite : poem

3. ZESTFUL : ENTHUSIASM ::
   (a) menial : work
   (b) acrid : smoke
   (c) negligent : vigilance
   (d) blithe : joy

4. STRAITS : HELP ::
   (a) sphere : shape
   (b) citrus : fruit
   (c) tedium : excitement
   (d) throng : congestion

5. ENDORSE : DISAPPROVE ::
   (a) initiate : begin
   (b) bestow : take
   (c) placate : gratify
   (d) smolder : burn

6. ABYSS : DITCH ::
   (a) sea : land
   (b) hole : open
   (c) mountain : hill
   (d) wound : doctor

7. ENLIGHTENED : IGNORANT ::
   (a) industrious : lazy
   (b) watchful : vigilant
   (c) precise : exact
   (d) irate : angry

8. VOCATIONAL : CAREER ::
   (a) aquatic : water
   (b) commit : crime
   (c) steal : bestow
   (d) borrow : money

9. MENAGERIE : ANIMALS ::
   (a) sky : clouds
   (b) theater : audience
   (c) ocean : ships
   (d) garden : plants

10. PLAUSIBLE : BELIEVABLE ::
    (a) stringent : strict
    (b) pretentious : humble
    (c) scrupulous : lax
    (d) preposterous : realistic

Bluegrass

To horse lovers, the word *bluegrass* **conjures** up a picture of Kentucky's **lush** blue-green pastures, home of champion racehorses; but to lovers of country music, bluegrass is the lively sound of fiddles, banjos, mandolins, and guitars playing together in rapid foot-stompin', hand-clappin' harmony. Its roots go back many years to the Scottish and Irish immigrants who settled in the Appalachian region. These settlers brought their traditional tunes and songs with them. In the days before television, movies, and radio, families were **obliged** to supply their own entertainment. Anyone who could scrape a tune from a fiddle or **warble** a song would be invited to join in.

After the Civil War, African Americans, freed from slavery, found jobs in Appalachia. They worked as coal miners, loggers, and railroad construction workers. They also introduced their music to the people of Appalachia, bringing in the "banjar," an African four-stringed instrument. The banjar was made from a hollowed gourd with a neck attached. Its twanging sound **complemented** the traditional fiddle so well that over time it was developed into the modern banjo. By the end of the nineteenth century, the guitar had been added, brought to Appalachia by city musicians traveling in bands through the region. All the **components** of bluegrass music were now in place. Its distinctive sound was beginning to emerge, although it did not yet have a name.

At first, the music coming out of Appalachia was ignored by most Americans, who criticized its lack of **subtlety.** They thought of it as music that would appeal only to **rustics.** This impression was often created by the musicians themselves. They enjoyed combining slapstick comedy with their musical **medleys.** The coming of radio in the 1920s put more **emphasis** on the music itself and brought it a wider audience and more general acceptance. Together with recorded music, radio offered greater commercial opportunities. Musicians were no longer content to play the fiddle or the guitar merely as a hobby. More and more began to make music their **vocation.** Among them was Bill Monroe, who was born in western Kentucky in 1911. Bill showed his **prowess** with the mandolin at an early age. In 1938, he formed a band and named it after the nickname of his native state—the Blue Grass Boys. Over the years that followed, the name of Monroe's band lent itself to the distinctive sound he had created. Monroe and his Blue Grass Boys continued to perform

| complement |
| component |
| conjure |
| emphasize |
| homage |
| impromptu |
| lush |
| medley |
| oblige |
| pretentious |
| prowess |
| rustic |
| subtle |
| vocation |
| warble |

until he was in his eighties, although he reduced the number of festival performances from 150 to 100 per year. On September 9, 1996, four days before his eighty-fifth birthday, Bill Monroe died.

Bluegrass festivals are held in just about every state in the union and in many foreign countries. These musical events are not at all **pretentious;** in fact, performers mix freely with their fans. Those attending enjoy taking out their own instruments to join in **impromptu** performances held in any open space between campers. Many also come to pay **homage** to Bill Monroe, the father of bluegrass.

▶ **Answer each of the following questions with a sentence. If a question does not contain a vocabulary word from the lesson's word list, use one in your answer. Use each word only once.**

1. Why is Kentucky a good place to raise horses?

_____

_____

2. At what stage of his life did Bill Monroe first show his musical ability?

_____

_____

3. Why do many fans take their instruments to bluegrass festivals?

_____

_____

4. Who would be especially welcome at Appalachian get-togethers in the days before radio and television?

_____

_____

5. Why did the banjo become popular in Appalachian music?

_____

_____

6. To lovers of country music, what does the name *bluegrass* suggest?

_____

_____

7. How would you describe a **medley** of Bill Monroe tunes?

_____

_____

8. What is the meaning of **obliged** as it is used in the passage?

_____

_____

9. What instruments are one **component** of bluegrass music?

_____

_____

10. Why are fans able to mix freely with musicians at bluegrass festivals?

_____

_____

11. What mistaken idea did some Americans have about the appeal of bluegrass music?

_____

_____

12. What criticism might some lovers of "fine" music make of bluegrass music?

_____

_____

| complement |
| component |
| conjure |
| emphasize |
| homage |
| impromptu |
| lush |
| medley |
| oblige |
| pretentious |
| prowess |
| rustic |
| subtle |
| vocation |
| warble |

13. Why do you think the bluegrass musicians ultimately eliminated the slapstick comedy routines?

_____

_____

14. How did Bill Monroe demonstrate his devotion to bluegrass music?

_____

_____

15. What special purpose drew bluegrass fans to Bill Monroe's performances?

_____

_____

Fun & Fascinating FACTS

- **Complement** is a noun and a verb. *Compliment* (with an *i*) is also a noun and a verb, but these two words have quite different meanings. A *compliment* is a remark that expresses praise, approval, or admiration. To *compliment* someone is to make such a remark.

- We sometimes refer to a person's profession, occupation, or chosen way of life as a *calling*. (Supreme Court Justice Ruth Bader Ginsburg has combined the *callings* of motherhood and the law.) *Calling* and **vocation** are synonyms, and this is no surprise because *vocation* comes from the Latin *vocare,* which means "to call." The prefix *a-* means "away from," and an *avocation* is a hobby or pastime, something done "away from" one's work or calling.

emphasize

verb To say or write something in a strong way to give it more importance or to make it more noticeable.

Word Family
de-**emphasize** (verb)
emphasis (noun)
emphatic (adjective)
emphatically (adverb)

Context Clues
These sentences give clues to the meaning of **emphasis.**

*Jorge's father was a teacher who **emphasized** the importance of a good education.*

*The writer underlined the word to **emphasize** it.*

Discussion & Writing Prompt
During a campaign, candidates for public office **emphasize** their good qualities. If you were running for student council, what qualities would you **emphasize,** and why?

2 min.	3 min.
1. Turn and talk to your partner or group.	2. Write 2–4 sentences.
Use this space to take notes or draw your ideas.	Be ready to share what you have written.

Study the definitions of the words. Then do the exercises that follow.

bounty
boun´ tē

n. 1. A payment made as a reward, especially one made by the authorities.
The town offered a $25 **bounty** for each predatory animal that was trapped.

2. That which is given freely, by nature or a generous person.
The people of Nova Scotia lived off the **bounty** of the sea.

bountiful *adj.* (boun´ ti fəl) Plentiful.
Farmers attributed the **bountiful** harvest to adequate rainfall throughout the growing season.

Talk with your partner about something your school has a bountiful supply of.

camouflage
kam´ ə fläzh

n. 1. The hiding of something as a result of its appearance.
The green color of a praying mantis is its natural means of **camouflage.**

2. Something used as a cover or disguise.
Netting covered with leafy branches provided **camouflage** for the trucks.

v. To hide or conceal, especially by disguising the appearance of.
Octopuses **camouflage** themselves by changing color to match their background.

Discuss with your partner what you could wear to provide you camouflage in a forest.

ebb
eb

v. 1. To recede, fall back, or pull away from.
The rocks near the shore were exposed as the tide **ebbed.**

2. To fall to a lower level or weaker state; to dwindle.
The patient's strength had **ebbed** to the point where getting out of bed was an effort.

n. The passing to a lower level or weaker state.
Just when the shipwrecked sailors' hopes of rescue were at their lowest **ebb,** they saw a ship approaching the island.

forage
fôr´ ij

v. To search for food or supplies.
We **foraged** in the forest for firewood.

n. Food such as hay or grain for farm animals.
I supplement the horses' **forage** with carrots and apples.

Chat with your partner about where wild animals might forage for food in the city.

| **harass** | *v.* 1. To trouble or annoy by attacking repeatedly. |
| hə ras´ | Swarms of mosquitoes **harassed** us as we left the tent. |

2. To cause to become worried or weary.
The store owners were **harassed** by the rapid increase in shoplifting.

Show your partner how you would act if a swarm of bees were harassing you.

| **insulate** | *v.* To cover with a material that keeps electricity, heat, or sound from escaping. |
| in´ sə lāt | The builder used fiberglass to **insulate** the walls. |

insulation *n.* Material that is used to insulate.
Their down provides geese with **insulation** against the cold.

| **lethargic** | *adj.* Slow moving; sleepy or tired. |
| lə thär´ jik | Extreme heat often makes people **lethargic.** |

lethargy *n.* (leth´ ər jē) A state of laziness, tiredness, or of not caring.
Despite repeated pep talks from the coach, a **lethargy** had settled over the team.

| **maneuver** | *n.* 1. A planned military movement. |
| mə nōō´ vər | A frontal attack on a well-defended position is not a **maneuver** I would recommend. |

2. A skillful move or clever trick.
Sacrificing her bishop early in the chess game turned out to be an effective **maneuver.**

v. 1. To perform military movements with.
General Lee **maneuvered** his forces so skillfully that the outcome of the battle was never in doubt.

2. To move or manage in a skillful way.
The tugboats **maneuvered** the ship into position alongside the dock.

Discuss with your partner the best way to maneuver through a crowded store.

| **mottled** | *adj.* Marked with different colored patches or blotches. |
| mät´ əld | The granite had a **mottled** pink and gray appearance. |

| **murky** | *adj.* Dark; gloomy. |
| mʉrk´ ē | I gazed over the side of the boat into the **murky** depths of the ocean. |

| **proximity** | *n.* The state of being close or next to; nearness. |
| präk sim´ ə tē | My family looked for a house with **proximity** to the school. |

Name three people in proximity to you and your partner.

| **replenish** | *v.* To fill up again. |
| rē plen´ ish | We **replenished** our water bottles at a little stream. |

Tell your partner where your family goes to replenish food supplies.

sleek	*adj.* 1. Smooth and glossy.
slēk	The dog's coat was **sleek** from daily brushing.
	2. Having slender, graceful lines.
	The **sleek** racing horse was a beautiful sight.

| **wary** | *adj.* On one's guard; watchful; suspicious. |
| wer´ ē | She advised me to be **wary** of the large crack in the sidewalk. |

wean	*v.* 1. To cause to stop depending on a mother's milk for nourishment.
wēn	Puppies are **weaned** at six weeks.
	2. To detach from something one has grown accustomed to.
	The cafeteria menu replaced doughnuts with a medley of fruits in an attempt to **wean** students away from sweets.

16A Using Words in Context

Read the following sentences. If the word in bold is used correctly, write C on the line. If the word is used incorrectly, write I on the line.

1. (a) Mr. Green **camouflaged** his name by adding an "e" to it. ___
   (b) Stick insects are masters of **camouflage,** as their name suggests. ___
   (c) Messages between the friends were **camouflaged** back and forth. ___
   (d) Before **camouflage** came into use, British soldiers went into battle wearing bright red uniforms. ___

2. (a) I **harassed** my older brother just because it annoyed him. ___
   (b) Windmills **harass** the power of the wind, turning it into electricity. ___
   (c) **Harassed** by doubts, she didn't know whether to leave or stay. ___
   (d) Flying monkeys **harassed** Dorothy on her way to Oz. ___

3. (a) **Lethargy** is one of the main symptoms of exhaustion. ___
   (b) Some people have a **lethargy** that prevents them from sleeping. ___
   (c) Akim is always **lethargic** first thing in the morning. ___
   (d) The food had become **lethargic** and had to be thrown out. ___

4. (a) I need to **replenish** my book. ___
   (b) The nomads **replenished** their water supply at the oasis. ___
   (c) The freezer **replenishes** the ice cubes automatically. ___
   (d) Anyone who disobeyed would be **replenished.** ___

5. (a) We felt **mottled** that he had ignored us. ___
   (b) The moth was invisible against the **mottled** background. ___
   (c) Dabbing with the paintbrush gives a **mottled** appearance to the paper. ___
   (d) I heard a **mottled** sound, and then there was silence. ___

6. (a) The annual flooding of the Nile gave Egypt **bountiful** harvests. ___
   (b) The **bounty** from the farm includes squash, cucumber, and tomatoes. ___
   (c) I put the **bounty** of paper in the folder. ___
   (d) There was a five-thousand-dollar **bounty** to find the rare bird. ___

7. (a) The tide began to **ebb** at 6:42 this morning. ___
   (b) Drops of water started to **ebb** from the ceiling. ___
   (c) Not a word **ebbed** from his mouth as he smiled secretly. ___
   (d) Rescue seemed unlikely, but hope never **ebbed** among the survivors. ___

8. (a) Roberto **maneuvered** his hand to his forehead and wiped sweat away. ___
   (b) **Maneuvering** a large herd of sheep is very difficult to do. ___
   (c) The skateboard **maneuver** ended in hilarious disaster. ___
   (d) Racecar drivers **maneuver** their cars to block others from taking
       the lead. ___

9. (a) A **wary** person is not easily fooled. ___
   (b) The **wary** fly avoided the spider web. ___
   (c) The explorers were **wary** of venturing too far into the jungle. ___
   (d) After marching for ten hours, we were too **wary** to do anything but sleep. ___

10. (a) The wildfires that **foraged** over a thousand acres are now under control. ___
    (b) I **foraged** through the coins in my pocket and took out a quarter. ___
    (c) Jieun searched the kitchen cupboards, **foraging** for something to eat. ___
    (d) **Forage** was dropped by helicopter to feed the cattle. ___

bounty
camouflage
ebb
forage
harass
insulate
lethargic
maneuver
mottled
murky
proximity
replenish
sleek
wary
wean

16B Making Connections

Circle the letter next to each correct answer. There may be more than one correct answer.

1. Which word or words go with *remove from?*
   (a) ebb   (b) wean   (c) detach   (d) insulate

2. Which word or words go with *suspicious?*
   (a) tranquil   (b) wary   (c) mottled   (d) inept

3. Which word or words go with *fill up?*
   (a) forage   (b) restore   (c) renovate   (d) replenish

4. Which word or words go with *movement?*
   (a) headlong   (b) hurtle   (c) maneuver   (d) insulate

5. Which word or words go with *protect?*
   (a) bounty   (b) insulate   (c) cocoon   (d) replenish

6. Which word or words go with *hard to see?*
   (a) proximity   (b) camouflaged   (c) murky   (d) shrouded

7. Which word or words go with *streamlined?*
   (a) murky   (b) lethargic   (c) sleek   (d) mottled

8. Which word or words go with *close?*
   (a) proximity   (b) bounty   (c) forage   (d) counterpart

9. Which word or words go with *plenty?*
   (a) abundant   (b) harvest   (c) bounty   (d) proximity

10. Which word or words go with *fall back?*
    (a) recede   (b) ebb   (c) ascend   (d) replenish

1. We were **harassed**
   (a) by a salesman as soon as we walked into the store.
   (b) into our soccer uniforms and ran onto the field.
   (c) by the school principal for being disrespectful.
   (d) by jellyfish as soon as we entered the water.

2. We were **insulated**
   (a) against the cold in our thick coats.
   (b) by our blankets and quilts.
   (c) when he accused us of cheating.
   (d) to keep from getting the flu.

3. I get **lethargic**
   (a) sometimes, so then I go for a brisk walk.
   (b) around eight o'clock in the evening.
   (c) reactions to certain kinds of food like peanuts.
   (d) when I think of the good times we used to have.

4. We **maneuvered**
   (a) the house until every room was spotless.
   (b) our way to the front of the line.
   (c) the pizza into six equal slices.
   (d) the boat to the dock.

5. The **mottled**
   (a) sound of scratching seemed to come from behind the wall.
   (b) wind blew cold through the valley.
   (c) look of granite was just what we wanted for the statue of the school mascot.
   (d) complexion told us he was embarrassed.

6. The **murkiness**
   (a) of the meal consisted of bread and cheese.
   (b) in the fog made it almost impossible to see anything.
   (c) of the water was not at all inviting.
   (d) in the sunshine made me very happy.

bounty
camouflage
ebb
forage
harass
insulate
lethargic
maneuver
mottled
murky
proximity
replenish
sleek
wary
wean

7. The **proximity**
   (a) of air in the lungs should be strong.
   (b) can be controlled by diet and exercise.
   (c) of my sister's face next to mine made me laugh.
   (d) of the apartment to the subway was why my dad chose to live there.

8. A **sleek**
   (a) coat on a dog looks smooth and soft.
   (b) limousine drove by us.
   (c) elephant rumbled across the path.
   (d) meal and a good night's sleep are what I need.

16D Completing Sentences

Complete the sentences to demonstrate your knowledge of the words in bold.

1. I feel **lethargic** when

   _____

2. I am **wary** of

   _____

3. To **forage** means to

   _____

4. If I'm out at night and want to **camouflage** myself, I could

   _____

5. If someone is **harassed,** that means

   _____

6. I would hate to be **weaned** off

   _____

7. A water glass needs to be **replenished** when

   _____

8. If your strength has **ebbed,** that means

   _____

9. **Insulation** is usually not needed in tropical countries because

   _____

10. **Proximity** to a hospital is important when

   _____ .

Harbor Seals

Because they live in close **proximity** to the shore, harbor seals are a familiar sight along the New England coast. You may have to look closely to see them because their coloring provides them with a good **camouflage;** their gray and black **mottled** coats are hard to see against the seaweed-covered rocks on which they spend much of their time. During the winter months, they inhabit the waters around Cape Cod and along the Massachusetts shoreline. Their dense fur and thick layer of blubber keep them so well **insulated** that in summer they seek the colder waters of Maine and the Atlantic provinces of Canada.

Harbor seals are equally at home on land and in the water. As the tide **ebbs,** they climb onto rocks along the shoreline. They return to the water at high tide to **forage** for crabs, fish, and squid. Harbor seals may seem **lethargic** as they lie basking in the sun, but actually they are **replenishing** their blood supply with fresh oxygen. Whether hunting for food or escaping from sharks and killer whales, harbor seals burn up oxygen rapidly when they are in the water.

Because of their **sleek** bodies and powerful rear flippers, harbor seals can swim up to fifteen miles an hour. They can also **maneuver** swiftly. They use their front flippers to brake and steer. Their excellent eyesight is necessary for survival. Harbor seals must watch for predators in the **murky** New England waters. Healthy harbor seals that stay out of harm's way can live for thirty years.

An adult harbor seal weighs over two hundred pounds and eats up to twenty pounds of fish a day. This makes the seals unpopular with those who fish for a living. In fact, seals were so unpopular in the 1800s that the state of Maine offered a **bounty** of five dollars for every harbor seal killed. Then the Marine Mammal Protection Act of 1972 made harbor seals a protected species. The Act was updated in 1994. It is now against the law to kill, capture, or **harass** them in any way.

Female harbor seals give birth in late May and early June. Newborn pups weigh about twenty pounds. They feed on their mother's milk until they are **weaned** at six to eight weeks. Within hours of being born, they are able to swim and are completely at home in the water. Young seals stay close to their

bounty
camouflage
ebb
forage
harass
insulate
lethargic
maneuver
mottled
murky
proximity
replenish
sleek
wary
wean

mothers. The mothers keep a **wary** eye on them until they are able to take care of themselves.

Some seals who run into problems can be seen by visitors to the New England Aquarium in Boston. Sick or injured seals that could not survive in the wild are brought there for medical treatment. They are kept in a holding tank outside the building. Once restored to health, the harbor seals are released into the ocean to enjoy its limitless freedom but also to face whatever dangers lurk there.

▶ **Answer each of the following questions with a sentence. If a question does not contain a vocabulary word from the lesson's word list, use one in your answer. Use each word only once.**

1. Why are harbor seals unlikely to be spotted in midocean?

_____

_____

2. What happens to the tide when it reaches the high-water mark?

_____

_____

3. Are harbor seals **lethargic** in the water?

_____

_____

4. Which single word describes both the body shape and coat of the harbor seal?

_____

_____

5. What is the meaning of **camouflage** as it is used in the passage?

_____

_____

6. Why do you need sharp eyes to see harbor seals basking on the rocks?

_____

_____

7. What is the meaning of **bounty** as it is used in the passage?

_____

_____

8. Why are harbor seals sometimes difficult to spot in the water?

_____

_____

9. Why do harbor seals spend so much time lying in the sun?

_____

_____

10. How does the passage show that seals are good mothers?

_____

_____

11. Why is it difficult for predators to catch harbor seals?

_____

_____

12. What is the purpose of the harbor seal's thick layer of blubber?

_____

_____

13. How do mature harbor seals obtain the nourishment they need?

_____

_____

14. How does the law protect harbor seals?

_____

_____

15. What is the meaning of **wean** as it is used in the passage?

_____

_____

| bounty |
| camouflage |
| ebb |
| forage |
| harass |
| insulate |
| lethargic |
| maneuver |
| mottled |
| murky |
| proximity |
| replenish |
| sleek |
| wary |
| wean |

Fun & Fascinating FACTS

- **Camouflage** is a French military term that has entered English while retaining its original French spelling and pronunciation.

- **Harass** is sometimes pronounced *ha rass'* and sometimes *har' ess*. While both pronunciations are correct, the second is considered preferable by many dictionaries.

- In some situations, **ebb** and *flow* are antonyms. For example, we speak of the *ebb and flow,* or falling and rising of the tide. (The science teacher explained that the tide *ebbs and flows* twice approximately every twenty-four hours.)

maneuver

noun A skillful action.

verb To move or turn skillfully, usually something large.

Context Clues

These sentences give clues to the meaning of **maneuver.**

The pilot's tricky **maneuvers** *delighted the spectators at the air show.*

The captain **maneuvered** *the enormous cruise ship into a tight spot at the dock.*

Word Parts

The root *man* means "hand." Another word with this root is *manipulate.*
Can you think of any other words with the root *man?*

Discussion & Writing Prompt

Describe a time when you witnessed someone skillfully **maneuver** a vehicle, such as a bus or a truck with a trailer.

2 min.	3 min.
1. Turn and talk to your partner or group.	**2.** Write 2–4 sentences.
Use this space to take notes or draw your ideas.	Be ready to share what you have written.

Review

Crossword Puzzle Solve the crossword puzzle by studying the clues and filling in the answer boxes. The number after a clue is the lesson the word is from.

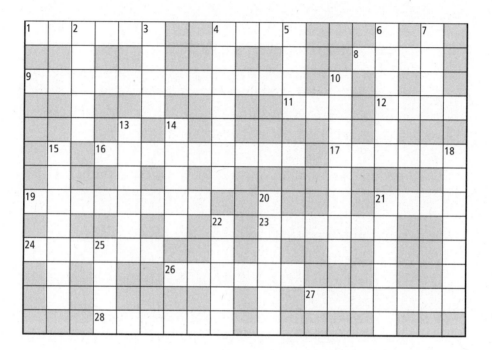

Clues Across

1. Extremely gloomy or depressing (14)
4. The _____ Canal is in Egypt.
8. On one's guard (16)
9. Too absurd to be believed (14)
11. Eight, nine, _____
12. In addition to; as well as
16. Producing wealth or profit (13)
17. Suggesting the country or country life (15)
19. One's occupation, trade, or career (15)
21. Sun, _____ , and stars
23. To do a favor for (15)
24. A mixture of dissimilar things (15)
26. The highest point (13)
27. To give one's backing to (13)
28. To start burning (13)

Clues Down

2. Glossy and smooth (16)
3. Growing thick and healthy (15)
4. Trouble or need (13)
5. Keen enjoyment (13)
6. To cause to become worried (16)
7. We see with them
10. Showing no fear (13)
13. Not easily seen or understood (15)
14. A bow and _____
15. Great skill or ability (15)
18. To make appear as if by magic (15)
20. Food for farm animals (16)
21. A wise friend and adviser (13)
22. Showing a childish lack of judgment (14)
25. To lie in wait as though about to attack (14)

Study the definitions of the words. Then do the exercises that follow.

appoint
ə point´

v. 1. To choose for an office or position.
The president **appoints** justices to the Supreme Court.

2. To set or decide upon.
Let's **appoint** a time for our next meeting.

appointment   *n.* 1. The act of appointing or being appointed.
All **appointments** to the Supreme Court must be approved by the Senate.

2. An arrangement or agreement to meet.
I made an **appointment** to see my teacher on Thursday.

Talk to your partner about the importance of regular dentist appointments.

assent
ə sent´

v. To give one's consent; to agree.
The principal **assented** to our proposal to wear jeans on Fridays.

n. An act of agreeing or acceptance.
My parents gave their **assent** to letting me go to the weekend sleepover.

Try to get your partner to assent to give you his or her lunch.

concur
kən kʉr´

v. To be in agreement.
Dr. Alvarez **concurred** with Dr. Yan's opinion that the patient did not require surgery.

consult
kən sult´

v. 1. To seek information or advice.
I **consulted** several reference books to get information about asteroids hitting Earth.

2. To talk things over in order to reach a decision.
While court went into recess, the lawyers **consulted** each other.

consultation   *n.* (kän səl tā´ shən) A discussion; a meeting to seek advice.
In my first **consultation** with the tutor, she gave me a positive approach to studying.

consultant   *n.* One whose advice is sought.
The city manager hired a **consultant** to advise her on care for the elderly.

Tell your partner whom you consult if you need help with math homework.

dissuade
di swād´

v. To prevent or discourage someone from doing something.
My friend **dissuaded** me from skiing the trail called White Heat.

Discuss with your partner how you could dissuade a friend from breaking a rule.

flabbergast
flab´ ər gast

v. To surprise so greatly that one is speechless; to amaze.
His preposterous story about being abducted by space aliens **flabbergasted** me.

haggle
hag´ əl

v. To argue about, especially about the price of something.
Mom **haggled** with the dealer for a while before agreeing on a price for the painting.

perturb
pər tʉrb´

v. To make uneasy; to upset greatly.
I was **perturbed** when our late departure caused me to miss my first class.

procure
prō kyoor´

v. To get by making an effort; to obtain.
By foraging in the woods, I was able to **procure** enough kindling to start a fire.

Chat with your partner about how students could procure the money for a trip to Washington, D.C.

receptive
rē sep´ tiv

adj. Ready and able to receive ideas or suggestions.
I told her I would be **receptive** to hearing her side of the story.

repudiate
rē pyōo´ dē āt

v. To refuse to support; to reject.
New discoveries often cause scientists to **repudiate** earlier beliefs.

resolve
rē zôlv´

v. 1. To make a firm promise to oneself.
I **resolve** to work even harder at my studies.

2. To solve.
We can **resolve** this little problem very easily.

n. A fixed purpose or intention.
The hard toil and long days weakened Mr. Sahir's **resolve** to finish the job.

Tell your partner how you might help resolve a fight between two friends.

signify
sig´ nə fī

v. 1. To be a sign of; to mean.
A nod of the head **signifies** agreement.

2. To make known or clear.
Signify your understanding by raising your hand.

significant *adj.* (sig nif´ ə kənt) Full of meaning; important.
"There was no forced entry. That is very **significant**," said the detective.

significance *n.* (sig nif´ ə kəns) Importance; meaning.
What is the **significance** of flying the flag upside down?

Show your partner a hand gesture that signifies "Good-bye."

sovereign	*adj.* 1. Highest; chief.
säv´rən	Creativity is a **sovereign** quality in fiction writing.
	2. Not controlled by others.
	After winning independence from England, the thirteen colonies formed a **sovereign** country.
	n. A king or queen; a monarch.
	The **sovereign's** portrait appears on all British postage stamps.
	sovereignty *n.* Freedom from political control by a foreign power.
	Poland regained its **sovereignty** when the Soviet Union collapsed at the end of the Cold War.

| trifling | *adj.* Of little value, importance, or meaning. |
| trī´fliŋ | Their objections to the plan are **trifling** and should be ignored. |

17A Finding Meanings

Choose two phrases to form a sentence that correctly uses a word from Word List 17. Then write the sentence.

1. (a) To repudiate something
   (b) To resolve something
   (c) is to settle it.
   (d) is to be the cause of it.

_____

_____

2. (a) To perturb someone is to
   (b) make that person uneasy.
   (c) To consult someone is to
   (d) reject that person.

_____

_____

3. (a) refuse to be bound by it.
   (b) sign one's name to it.
   (c) To procure an agreement is to
   (d) To repudiate an agreement is to

_____

_____

4. (a) An appointment is
   (b) A consultation is
   (c) a matter of little importance.
   (d) the naming of a person to a position.

_____

_____

| appoint |
| assent |
| concur |
| consult |
| dissuade |
| flabbergast |
| haggle |
| perturb |
| procure |
| receptive |
| repudiate |
| resolve |
| signify |
| sovereign |
| trifling |

5. (a) is to be a sign of change.
   (b) is to be unwilling to accept change.
   (c) To assent to change
   (d) To signify change

_____

_____

6. (a) A trifling figure is one
   (b) that has no real existence.
   (c) A sovereign figure is one
   (d) that stands out above all others.

_____

_____

7. (a) be unable to make up one's mind.
   (b) To concur is to
   (c) be in agreement.
   (d) To haggle is to

_____

_____

8. (a) To flabbergast someone
   (b) is to welcome that person.
   (c) To dissuade someone
   (d) is to amaze that person.

_____

_____

9. (a) is to give it up.
   (b) is to obtain it.
   (c) To procure something
   (d) To assent to something

_____

_____

10. (a) Someone who is dissuaded
    (b) Someone who is receptive
    (c) is ready to accept new ideas.
    (d) is unwilling to consider new ideas.

_____

_____

17B Just the Right Word

Replace each phrase in bold with a single word (or form of the word) from the word list.

1. I was able to **obtain through my own efforts** forage for the horses.

2. My parents' reasonable objections weakened my **firm intention** to join the club.

3. Belize, formerly British Honduras, gained **freedom from political control by another country** in 1981.

4. The **meeting in which I talked things over** with the doctor lasted thirty minutes.

5. I **indicated that I was willing to give my approval** to the plan.

6. Let's not waste our time on such **completely unimportant** matters.

7. A vote of nine to zero **makes it clear** that the decision was unanimous.

8. My mom paid what the car salesperson asked because she was unwilling to **argue over the price.**

9. We tried to **use my powers of persuasion in order to prevent** them from driving in such icy conditions.

10. All the relatives gathered in the lawyer's office for the **meeting that had been arranged the week before.**

| appoint |
| assent |
| concur |
| consult |
| dissuade |
| flabbergast |
| haggle |
| perturb |
| procure |
| receptive |
| repudiate |
| resolve |
| signify |
| sovereign |
| trifling |

17c Applying Meanings

Circle the letter or letters next to each correct answer. There may be more than one correct answer.

1. Which of the following would result in a country's loss of **sovereignty?**
   - (a) It closes off its borders.
   - (b) It abolishes its army.
   - (c) It is overrun by a foreign power.
   - (d) Its citizens overthrow the ruler.

2. Which of the following might a person **resolve** to do?
   - (a) drive more carefully
   - (b) catch a cold
   - (c) go to bed earlier
   - (d) fail a test

3. Which of the following might be **haggled** over?
   - (a) the terms of an agreement
   - (b) the price of an antique
   - (c) the day on which Thanksgiving falls
   - (d) the number of feet in a mile

4. Which of the following might **perturb** a businessperson?
   - (a) increased competition
   - (b) increased taxes
   - (c) increased profits
   - (d) increased expenses

5. Which of the following are ways of **assenting?**
   - (a) nodding one's head
   - (b) saying yes
   - (c) saying no
   - (d) shaking one's head

6. Which of the following could be **appointed?**
   - (a) a club president
   - (b) a Supreme Court judge
   - (c) a place to meet
   - (d) a winter storm

7. Which of the following have **significance?**
   - (a) a hurricane
   - (b) lethargy after a large meal
   - (c) a presidential election
   - (d) the color of one's eyes

8. Which of the following can be **consulted?**
   - (a) a dictionary
   - (b) a mentor
   - (c) an authority
   - (d) an accountant

In each sentence, use the boldfaced word (or words) to help identify the Latin word that completes the sentence. You may need to combine the Latin word with a prefix. The number after each item is the lesson the word is from.

Prefixes
com- (together)
in- (not)
inter- (between)
re- (again)
sub- (under)

Latin Words
mergere (to plunge)   *vincere* (to conquer)
plenus (full)   *placare* (to calm)
proximus (near)   *ponere* (to put)
trepidus (afraid)   *venire* (to come)

1. Several of these **put together** make a whole.
   They are _____. (15)

2. This is what you do to **calm** hurt feelings.
   You _____ someone. (9)

3. Can't be **conquered?**
   You are _____! (9)

4. Diving **under** the surface?
   You're going to _____ yourself. (11)

5. You're getting **near** the park.
   You're in _____ to it now! (16)

6. You can **fill** your tank **again.**
   The word is _____. (16)

7. Don't want to **come between** friends?
   Then don't _____. (12)

8. Don't be **afraid!**
   Be _____. (13)

| appoint |
| assent |
| concur |
| consult |
| dissuade |
| flabbergast |
| haggle |
| perturb |
| procure |
| receptive |
| repudiate |
| resolve |
| signify |
| sovereign |
| trifling |

"A Noble Bargain"

Throughout history, countries that have extended their borders have done so mainly by military conquest; the United States is one of the few nations that has ever done so by purchase. In one of the greatest bargains ever made, it **procured** almost a million square miles at a cost of just over fifteen million dollars.

In 1802, the **sovereignty** of the United States ended at the Mississippi River. France had a legal claim to all the land beyond it as far as the Rocky Mountains. United States shipping on the Mississippi passed through New Orleans, Louisiana, on its way to the sea. President Thomas Jefferson was **perturbed** by the possibility that France might close off the river. To prevent this, he **resolved** to buy New Orleans, together with western Florida, from the French.

Certain conditions were in Jefferson's favor. France was on the verge of war with Britain and, therefore, needed money. Should the British attack New Orleans, the French would, Jefferson believed, have difficulty defending it. It made sense to conclude that France would prefer the territory go to America rather than to Britain.

To pursue his plan, Jefferson **appointed** two agents to represent the United States. These agents met with the French foreign minister in France to discuss the purchase. He proposed that the United States buy all the land from the Mississippi to the Rockies, a total of almost a million square miles. The two Americans were **flabbergasted** but **receptive** to the idea. Congress had approved spending only two million dollars; however, the cost would now greatly exceed that amount. After a considerable amount of **haggling**, a price of fifteen million dollars was finally agreed on. The French foreign minister commented at the time the deal was struck that the United States had made "a noble bargain."

Members of Congress did not **concur** with this view and wanted to **repudiate** the agreement with France. They thought that fifteen million dollars was an excessive amount to pay. They were also upset that the president's agents had agreed to the French offer without **consulting** them. President Jefferson appeared before Congress in an attempt to **dissuade** its members from voting against the purchase. He pointed out that the United

States would be doubled in size by the transaction. He also stated that if the United States did not act promptly, the French might withdraw their offer. Somewhat grudgingly, Congress gave its **assent** to the "Louisiana Purchase." A year later the United States flag was raised in New Orleans, **signifying** the end of France's involvement in North America.

Just how good a bargain was the Louisiana Purchase? Iowa farmland in 2003 sold for about $2,500 an acre. The six hundred million acres of land the United States bought in 1803 had cost the **trifling** sum of two and a half cents an acre.

▶ **Answer each of the following questions with a sentence. If a question does not contain a vocabulary word from the lesson's word list, use one in your answer. Use each word only once.**

1. Why is 1803 a **significant** date in French history?

_____

_____

2. How did Jefferson feel about the possibility that France might close off the Mississippi River?

_____

_____

3. Why would it be incorrect to call Florida a **sovereign** state in 1802?

_____

_____

4. What decision did Jefferson make to ensure that the Mississippi River stayed open?

_____

_____

5. Did Jefferson himself deal directly with the French?

_____

_____

6. Were members of Congress happy about the deal with the French?

_____

_____

| appoint |
| assent |
| concur |
| consult |
| dissuade |
| flabbergast |
| haggle |
| perturb |
| procure |
| receptive |
| repudiate |
| resolve |
| signify |
| sovereign |
| trifling |

7. How do you know that the French proposal was unexpected?

_____

_____

8. How did the Americans make sure they paid no more than necessary?

_____

_____

9. What is the meaning of **receptive** as it is used in the passage?

_____

_____

10. How much land did the United States purchase from France?

_____

_____

11. What was the cost per acre of the Louisiana Purchase?

_____

_____

12. Did all members of Congress agree that the two Americans had performed a great service?

_____

_____

13. What was the purpose of Jefferson's address to the members of Congress?

_____

_____

14. What would have happened if Congress had **repudiated** the agreement?

_____

_____

15. What was Congress's response to Jefferson's appeal?

_____

_____

Fun & Fascinating FACTS

- The antonym of **assent** is *dissent;* its homophone is *ascent,* "the act of climbing or ascending."

- The noun formed from the verb **resolve** is *resolution*—one may *resolve* to do something; one may also make a *resolution* to do something. *Resolve* is also a noun, and its meaning overlaps somewhat with *resolution. Resolve* is a state of mind and means "firmness of purpose." (Nothing could shake her *resolve* to be a doctor.) A *resolution* is a statement of purpose, made to oneself or to others, concerning a course of action. (I made a New Year's *resolution* to exercise every day.) *Resolution* also means "an explanation or a solution." (The *resolution* of the mystery is withheld until the end of the novel.)

- **Sovereign** is formed from the Latin *super,* which means "over" or "above." As a noun, *sovereign* is a synonym for *monarch,* and the fact that a monarch *reigns* influenced the present form and spelling of the word. The noun formed from the adjective is *sovereignty.* (By world agreement, no country may claim *sovereignty* over Antarctica.)

  A *sovereign* is also a British gold coin no longer in use; the first ones were struck in 1489 and bore a likeness of the English king Henry VII.

- The noun *trifle* is related to the adjective **trifling.** A *trifle* is something of little value or importance; it is also a sum of money so small as to be of no account. *Trifle* is also a verb that means "to talk or deal with in an insincere way." (Only an unscrupulous person would *trifle* with someone's affections.)

appoint
assent
concur
consult
dissuade
flabbergast
haggle
perturb
procure
receptive
repudiate
resolve
signify
sovereign
trifling

Vocabulary Extension

resolve

verb 1. To make a decision to do something.

2. To find a way to deal with a problem.

noun Determination to succeed.

I **resolved** to clean my room before dinner.

Context Clues

These sentences give clues to the meaning of **resolve.**

Rian **resolved** to learn everything he could about computer coding.

It took a couple days, but the sisters **resolved** their argument.

He was so tired he almost quit the race, but Carson found the **resolve** to finish strong.

Discussion & Writing Prompt

Describe a time you had a disagreement with a friend. How did you **resolve** things?

2 min.	3 min.
1. Turn and talk to your partner or group.	**2.** Write 2–4 sentences.
Use this space to take notes or draw your ideas.	Be ready to share what you have written.

Study the definitions of the words. Then do the exercises that follow.

acclaim
ə klām´

v. To praise strongly or applaud loudly.
Audiences **acclaimed** the new student play.

n. Strong praise or loud applause; approval.
The musicians from China won the critic's **acclaim** last night at Symphony Hall.

bigot
big´ ət

n. One who is not tolerant of those people who are different in some way; a prejudiced person.
Only a **bigot** would claim that one race is superior to another.

bigotry *n.* The intolerant attitude or behavior of such a person.
In one of their songs, the Beatles asked listeners to imagine a world free of **bigotry.**

Discuss with your partner whether you could be a friend to a bigot.

covet
kuv´ ət

v. To have a strong and envious desire for, especially for something belonging to another.
The little girl **coveted** her teacher's blue notebook.

coveted *adj.* Greatly prized; highly desired.
Former President Jimmy Carter won the **coveted** Nobel Peace Prize in 2002.

deceased
dē sēst´

adj. Dead, with regard to a person.
The man's thoughts often turned to his **deceased** wife.

n. (with *the*) One who has died recently.
The funeral director asked if I was a relative of the **deceased.**

formidable
fôr´ mə də bəl

adj. 1. Causing fear or apprehension.
A team with a fourteen-game winning streak is a **formidable** opponent.

2. Difficult.
Crossing the Rocky Mountains was a **formidable** task for settlers heading west.

Tell your partner about a formidable task you completed, such as babysitting small children or cleaning out the garage.

ghetto
get´ ō

n. A section of a city occupied by a minority group of people, usually because of poverty or social pressure.
The Warsaw **ghetto** in Poland was the location of the largest uprising during World War II.

momentous
mō men´ təs

adj. Very important.
The day of high school graduation is a **momentous** one for students.

Chat with your partner about what you think are the momentous responsibilities of being a parent.

oppress
ə pres´

v. 1. To weigh down with worry.
Fear of the difficult math exam **oppressed** the students.

2. To keep down by severe and unjust use of force.
Peasants **oppressed** by the monarchy became the leaders of the French Revolution.

oppression *n.* (ə presh´ ən) The act or state of being oppressed.
The **oppression** of African Americans led to the Civil Rights Movement of the 1950s and '60s.

oppressive *adj.* Very harsh or burdensome.
This **oppressive** heat makes one very lethargic.

Talk with your partner about how it would feel to live under oppression.

overwhelm
ō vər hwelm´

v. 1. To defeat utterly and completely.
Sioux and Cheyenne warriors **overwhelmed** General Custer's army at the Battle of Little Big Horn in 1876.

2. To deeply affect the mind or emotions of.
We were **overwhelmed** by the welcome we received.

3. To upset; to turn over.
A huge wave **overwhelmed** the small boat.

overwhelming *adj.* Great in strength or effect.
The student bake sale was an **overwhelming** success.

Share with your partner events or places that are overwhelming to you.

perceive
pər sēv´

v. 1. To become aware of through the senses, especially the sense of sight.
I **perceived** a figure in the distance but could not make out who it was.

2. To take in information through the mind.
I **perceived** a subtle shift in their attitude.

perception *n.* (pər sep´ shən) The act of perceiving or the thing perceived.
Because I am farsighted, my **perception** of close objects is slightly fuzzy.

Discuss with your partner how witnesses can have different perceptions of the same event.

premiere
prē mir´

n. The first showing of a play, film, etc.
The play, a big success in London, has its North American **premiere** this Saturday.

| **prospective** | *adj.* Expected or likely to happen or become. |
| prä spek´ tiv | The **prospective** bride and groom want to have a June wedding. |

Tell your partner a nice thing to say to a prospective graduate.

| **spurn** | *v.* To refuse in a scornful way. |
| spu̇rn | I **spurned** their offer of help because there were too many conditions attached to it. |

| **staunch** | *adj.* Faithful; true; strong. |
| stônch | Mr. Fielding, a **staunch** supporter of Little League baseball, donated the uniforms for our team. |

theme	*n.* 1. A dominant idea, as in art, literature, or music; a topic or subject.
thēm	The **theme** of the story is the danger of excessive pride.
	2. A short essay on a single subject.
	I had to write a **theme** on ambition.
	3. A series of musical notes on which variations are made; a melody that is associated with a film or television show.
	The concert began with a medley of **themes** from popular television shows.

18A Using Words in Context

Read the following sentences. If the word in bold is used correctly, write C on the line. If the word is used incorrectly, write I on the line.

1. (a) Minority groups around the world have frequently been **oppressed.** ___
   (b) The **oppressive** climate of the tropics makes people lethargic. ___
   (c) The woman fell into a deep **oppression** when her dog was lost. ___
   (d) The **oppression** in the road has been filled in. ___

2. (a) The huge tidal wave **overwhelmed** the barriers. ___
   (b) I was **overwhelmed** by their generosity. ___
   (c) Ashraf **overwhelmed** the test, scoring one hundred percent. ___
   (d) The army achieved an **overwhelming** victory to end the war. ___

3. (a) I am **perceived** as shallow by people who don't know me. ___
   (b) I **perceived** a glimmer of hope, even though things looked dismal. ___
   (c) **Perceptions** can change as we learn more about a person. ___
   (d) To **perceive** an award, you must win the science fair. ___

4. (a) Fish can be **acclaimed** from the sea. ___

   (b) In colonial times, if you settled on land, you could **acclaim** it as your own. ___

   (c) The teacher was **acclaimed** as the best in the school. ___

   (d) Not everyone joined in the **acclaim** for the president. ___

5. (a) The **theme** on the jacket is torn and needs to be fixed. ___

   (b) The **theme** park is dedicated to famous cartoon characters. ___

   (c) The **theme** of Hollywood gangster movies is that crime does not pay. ___

   (d) The **theme** of the costume party was "kings and queens." ___

6. (a) A **bigot** is prejudiced against people because of their religion or country of origin. ___

   (b) Political candidates who defend **bigotry** do not deserve our votes. ___

   (c) The mechanic replaced the **bigot** on the wheel. ___

   (d) The **bigotry** on the blanket makes it very soft. ___

7. (a) Mariángel won a **coveted** position on the swim team. ___

   (b) Alec looked down into the **coveted,** stinky, slimy sewer. ___

   (c) I **coveted** my shoes after the concert and fell into bed. ___

   (d) She couldn't help but **covet** her friend's vacation to Hawaii. ___

8. (a) A **formidable** cheer greeted the announcement that school was canceled. ___

   (b) Taking on a professional was a **formidable** task for the inexperienced challenger. ___

   (c) We face **formidable** problems if we expect to run the whole way. ___

   (d) The Mojave Desert was a **formidable** obstacle for the wagon train. ___

9. (a) John Glenn's flight was a **momentous** event in space history. ___

   (b) The **momentous** breeze wasn't very strong at all. ___

   (c) Rebuilding the school involved **momentous** challenges. ___

   (d) This was no surprise, as it has happened **momentous** times before. ___

10. (a) **Prospective** sites for the new hospital are being looked at. ___

    (b) **Prospective** members were questioned closely about their interests. ___

    (c) Seen from outer space, **prospective** Earth is a tiny dot. ___

    (d) Look at the **prospective** peas on your plate. ___

18B Making Connections

Circle the letter next to each correct answer. There may be more than one correct answer.

1. Which word or words go with *poverty?*
   (a) hovel
   (b) sovereign
   (c) ghetto
   (d) covet

2. Which word or words go with *theater?*
   (a) entertain
   (b) premiere
   (c) debut
   (d) prospective

3. Which word or words go with *refuse?*
   (a) replenish
   (b) repudiate
   (c) acclaim
   (d) spurn

4. Which word or words go with *loyal?*
   (a) staunch
   (b) deceased
   (c) steadfast
   (d) prospective

5. Which word or words go with *death?*
   (a) premiere
   (b) fatality
   (c) slaughter
   (d) deceased

6. Which word or words go with *praise?*
   (a) theme
   (b) acclaim
   (c) bigotry
   (d) esteem

7. Which word or words go with *desire?*
   (a) covet
   (b) spurn
   (c) perceive
   (d) crave

8. Which word or words go with *defeat?*
   (a) acclaim
   (b) vanquish
   (c) rout
   (d) overwhelm

9. Which word or words go with *powerful?*
   (a) deceased
   (b) formidable
   (c) prospective
   (d) wary

10. Which word or words go with *intolerance?*
   (a) bigotry
   (b) camouflage
   (c) oppression
   (d) prejudice

acclaim
bigot
covet
deceased
formidable
ghetto
momentous
oppress
overwhelm
perceive
premiere
prospective
spurn
staunch
theme

18C Determining Meanings

Circle the letter next to each answer choice that correctly completes the sentence. There may be more than one correct answer.

1. The **deceased**
   (a) are too great in number to count after the earthquake.
   (b) were laid to rest in the local cemetery.
   (c) number of games on the shelves was disappointing.
   (d) sand stuck to my feet and ankles at the beach.

2. A **ghetto**
   (a) is a lizard with a long tail.
   (b) was established in many European cities in the 1940s.
   (c) in Lithuania housed forty thousand Jewish people who were forced to live there during the war.
   (d) can be found deep under the ocean's surface.

3. The **oppressiveness** of
   (a) this heat makes it hard to breathe.
   (b) the leader's rule was very difficult to live with.
   (c) all the wonderfully cool air is wonderful.
   (d) each flower grew all over the meadow.

4. **Perceiving**
   (a) what is true and what is false is important for a judge.
   (b) things from a shop is against the law.
   (c) the difference between what is real and what is fake should be easy.
   (d) softly down the path was a Bengal tiger.

5. The **premiere**
   (a) in the book is on white paper.
   (b) is the counterpart of the ocean.
   (c) of the movie was incredibly crowded.
   (d) of the play was unfortunately not very successful.

6. You might **spurn**
   (a) offers that seem too good to be true.
   (b) that scrap metal into something useful.
   (c) teachers who don't care whether you learn.
   (d) junk food if you are trying to be healthy.

7. A **staunch**

   (a) was driven into the ground to mark the spot.

   (b) friend helped me through some difficult times.

   (c) rope kept the boat tied to the dock.

   (d) supporter of the president will vote for her again.

8. The **theme**

   (a) of a certain popular movie was played at the end of the concert.

   (b) of the book is to always be true to who you are.

   (c) huddled before the first play of the game.

   (d) in television shows often has to do with family togetherness.

18D Completing Sentences

Complete the sentences to demonstrate your knowledge of the words in bold.

acclaim
bigot
covet
deceased
formidable
ghetto
momentous
oppress
overwhelm
perceive
premiere
prospective
spurn
staunch
theme

1. A **momentous** event might be

   _____.

2. I try not to get **overwhelmed** by

   _____.

3. Something **formidable** I have faced is

   _____.

4. My **perception** about my friends is

   _____.

5. Someone worthy of **acclaim** is

   _____.

6. If someone **spurns** my help, I would feel

   _____.

7. I am a **staunch** believer in

   _____.

8. To **covet** something is to

   _____.

9. My favorite musical **theme** from a movie or TV show is

   _____.

10. If you feel **oppressed,** that means you

   _____.

Vocabulary in Context

Read the passage.

An American Classic

When Lorraine Hansberry's play *A Raisin in the Sun* opened in New York on March 11, 1959, it was a **momentous** day in the history of the American theater. *A Raisin in the Sun* was the first play written by an African American woman to appear on Broadway. It opened up the American theater to African Americans and broadened people's **perceptions** of the African American experience in society.

The reviews were **overwhelmingly** favorable. Even its **staunchest** supporters could not have predicted the impact the play would have on the American theater. It went on to win the **coveted** New York Drama Critics Circle award for Best Play of the Year. The opposition for the award was **formidable,** including works by two of America's greatest playwrights, Tennessee Williams and Eugene O'Neill.

A Raisin in the Sun is about African Americans confronting **oppression** in their daily lives, a **theme** that Hansberry was painfully familiar with in her own life. In 1938, her parents bought a house in an all-white neighborhood. The **bigotry** of their new neighbors resulted in a legal battle over property rights. A lower court ordered the Hansberrys to move out. They fought the case all the way to the U.S. Supreme Court and won, but the family suffered terribly in the process. Prejudice quickly escalated into violence. When Lorraine was eight years old, she was almost killed by a concrete slab, thrown by an angry neighbor, that narrowly missed her head.

Hansberry's play tells the story of Lena Younger, who has received ten thousand dollars from her recently **deceased** husband's life insurance. Her dream is to move her family of five out of their cramped and rundown apartment in Chicago's South Side **ghetto.** She wants to use the money to buy a home in a white neighborhood, but doing that is not so simple.

Mrs. Younger is pressured by her son Walter to give him the money to improve his own financial state. Walter wants to invest in a store. At the same time, her daughter Beneatha needs money; her dream is to attend medical school. Mrs. Younger decides to try to keep the family together by making a down payment on a house with about one-third of the money. She gives the remaining sum to Walter under the condition that he set aside $3,000 for his sister's tuition; the rest he may use as he wishes.

Before the family moves in, a **prospective** white neighbor contacts Mrs. Younger and explains that he is speaking for the entire neighborhood. He offers to buy back the house at a handsome profit for Mrs. Younger. Recognizing the offer as one motivated by blatant racism, she **spurns** it.

Matters soon get even more complicated. The family learns that Walter's business partner has cheated him out of the remaining money. The amount that was supposed to go toward Beneatha's education is gone.

The play ends with Mrs. Younger holding firm against all pressures and finding the courage to face new ones. The family will move into the all-white neighborhood, with all its problems, dangers, and opportunities.

A Raisin in the Sun ran for 533 performances on Broadway. Touring companies took it all over America, offering opportunities for African American actors on a scale never known before. African Americans turned out in huge numbers to see a major American play that addressed the plight of minorities trying to improve their lives. In 2014, fifty-five years after its Broadway **premiere,** the play was revived on Broadway with Denzel Washington starring as Walter. The revival won universal **acclaim** and established *A Raisin in the Sun* as an American classic.

▶ **Answer each of the following questions with a sentence. If a question does not contain a vocabulary word from the lesson's word list, use one in your answer. Use each word only once.**

acclaim
bigot
covet
deceased
formidable
ghetto
momentous
oppress
overwhelm
perceive
premiere
prospective
spurn
staunch
theme

1. In what year did *A Raisin in the Sun* open on Broadway?

_____

_____

2. What effect did *A Raisin in the Sun* have on people?

_____

_____

3. What is the meaning of **theme** as it is used in the passage?

_____

_____

4. Why was March 11, 1959, a **momentous** day in the history of the American theater?

_____

_____

5. What important award did the play win?

_____

_____

6. Why must winning the award have given Lorraine Hansberry special satisfaction?

_____

_____

7. Were the reviews of the play positive or negative?

_____

_____

8. What might **staunch** supporters of the play have done to help it succeed?

_____

_____

9. Why is the person making the offer to buy the house from Mrs. Younger described as a **prospective** neighbor?

_____

_____

10. How does the passage show that Mrs. Younger scorns the offer?

_____

_____

11. What sort of person is the neighor who offers to buy back the house from Mrs. Younger?

_____

_____

12. How does Mrs. Younger deal with the **oppression** she encounters?

_____

_____

13. Why does Mr. Younger not appear in the play?

_____

_____

14. Why were many African Americans able to identify with the play's message?

_____

_____

15. What status had the play achieved by 2014?

_____

_____

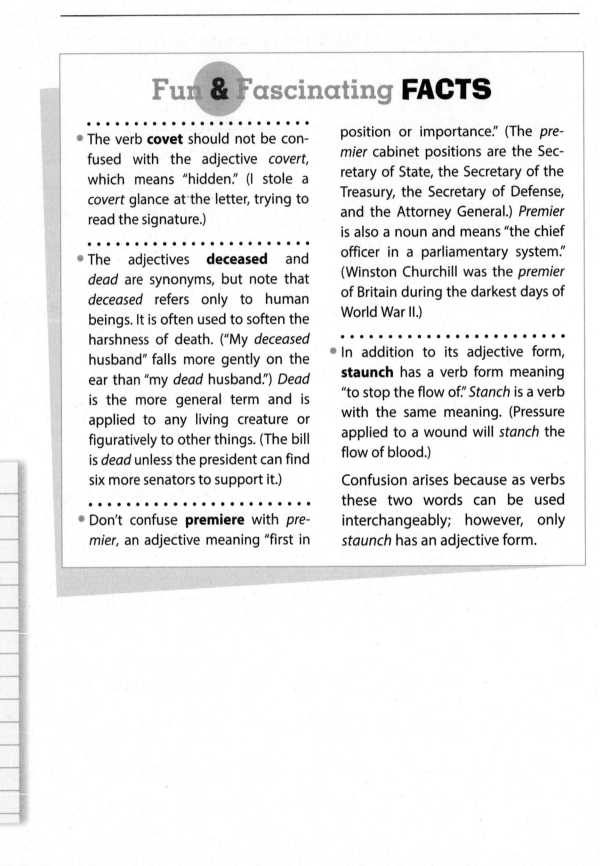

Fun & Fascinating FACTS

- The verb **covet** should not be confused with the adjective *covert*, which means "hidden." (I stole a *covert* glance at the letter, trying to read the signature.)

- The adjectives **deceased** and *dead* are synonyms, but note that *deceased* refers only to human beings. It is often used to soften the harshness of death. ("My *deceased* husband" falls more gently on the ear than "my *dead* husband.") *Dead* is the more general term and is applied to any living creature or figuratively to other things. (The bill is *dead* unless the president can find six more senators to support it.)

- Don't confuse **premiere** with *premier*, an adjective meaning "first in position or importance." (The *premier* cabinet positions are the Secretary of State, the Secretary of the Treasury, the Secretary of Defense, and the Attorney General.) *Premier* is also a noun and means "the chief officer in a parliamentary system." (Winston Churchill was the *premier* of Britain during the darkest days of World War II.)

- In addition to its adjective form, **staunch** has a verb form meaning "to stop the flow of." *Stanch* is a verb with the same meaning. (Pressure applied to a wound will *stanch* the flow of blood.)

Confusion arises because as verbs these two words can be used interchangeably; however, only *staunch* has an adjective form.

acclaim
bigot
covet
deceased
formidable
ghetto
momentous
oppress
overwhelm
perceive
premiere
prospective
spurn
staunch
theme

perceive

verb 1. To become aware of through the senses.

2. To understand about someone or recognize something without being told or shown.

*I **perceived** my dog's eyes shining out of the night in the backyard.*

Word Family

perceivable (adjective)
perceivably (adverb)
perceiver (noun)
perception (noun)
perceptive (adjective)

Context Clues

These sentences give clues to the meaning of **perceive**.

*Luke could **perceive** a kitten's faint meow coming from under the porch.*

*Renata was saying cheery things, but her friends **perceived** a hint of disappointment in her voice.*

Discussion & Writing Prompt

How might a person **perceive** the world if he or she is visually impaired?

2 min.	3 min.
1. Turn and talk to your partner or group.	2. Write 2–4 sentences.
Use this space to take notes or draw your ideas.	Be ready to share what you have written.

Study the definitions of the words. Then do the exercises that follow.

adverse
ad vʉrs´

adj. 1. Working against; serving to oppose.
The response to the proposed year-round school was so **adverse** that the school board dropped the idea.

2. Harmful; unfavorable.
Some people have an **adverse** reaction to aspirin.

Share with your partner a time when you had an adverse reaction, such as to food or a bug bite.

aloof
ə lo͞of´

adj. Remote or distant, usually by choice; showing no interest.
His **aloof** manner kept us from becoming close friends.

adv. In an aloof manner.
Although he sat with the group, he stayed **aloof** from the discussion they were having.

alternative
ôl tʉr´ nə tiv

adj. Allowing a choice between two or more things.
There is an **alternative** route you could take to get to town, but it's a bit longer.

n. 1. A choice between two or more things.
Your **alternatives** are to come with us or stay home.

2. Any one of the things that can be chosen.
I chose the second **alternative** and stayed home.

Talk to your partner about the alternatives young people have after finishing high school.

canine
kā´ nīn

adj. Of, or relating to, dogs or related animals.
Wolves, foxes, dogs, jackals, and coyotes are members of the **canine** family.

n. A member of the canine family.
I take my Old English sheepdog to a groomer who specializes in large **canines.**

compulsory
kəm pul´ sər ē

adj. Required by law or a firm rule.
Training is **compulsory** for all lifeguards.

consecutive
kən sek´ yo͞o tiv

adj. Following one after another in order.
It rained for five **consecutive** days last week.

Name three consecutive letters from the alphabet, and then have your partner say the next consecutive letter.

desolate
des´ ə lət

adj. 1. Deserted; lonely; without signs of life.
There was not even a gas station on the **desolate** stretch of highway.

2. Filled with sorrow.
The children were **desolate** when the kitten got lost in the woods.

dispatch
di spach´

v. 1. To send on specific business.
The senator **dispatched** an aide to meet with reporters.

2. To finish or complete promptly.
Zion **dispatched** the entire plate of spaghetti before we had tucked in our napkins.

3. To kill quickly.
The fly was **dispatched** with a single blow.

n. (dis´ pach) 1. Speed in movement or performance.
You must act with **dispatch** if you hope to settle the matter by noon tomorrow.

2. A written message sent quickly.
A motorcyclist carried the **dispatches** to the address.

Explain to your partner a situation in which you would want to dispatch someone to do something you don't want to do.

distinction
di stiŋk´ shən

n. 1. A recognition of the way things differ.
The lunchroom makes a **distinction** between the regular menu and the gluten-free menu.

2. Special honor or regard.
Astronaut John Glenn had the **distinction** of being the first American to orbit Earth.

3. Excellence of performance or ability.
Amina served as class president with **distinction.**

Chat with your partner about the distinction between night and day.

endure
en door´

v. 1. To put up with; to bear.
The pioneers who headed west had to **endure** incredible hardship along the way.

2. To go on for a long time; to last.
Despite occasional quarrels, my grandparents' marriage **endured** for over fifty years.

endurance *n.* The ability to put up with hardship; the quality of putting up with hardship.
There is no better test of a runner's **endurance** than the marathon.

Discuss with your partner a physical activity that tests your endurance.

fluctuate fluk´ chŏŏ āt	*v.* To rise and fall; to keep changing. The supply of fresh vegetables **fluctuates** with the seasons. **fluctuation** *n.* A rising and falling movement. In the Midwest, wide temperature **fluctuations** are to be expected in October. *Share with your partner something that makes your emotions fluctuate.*
grueling grōō´ əl iŋ	*adj.* Tiring; exhausting. Mount Washington is a **grueling** climb for most hikers.
maul môl	*v.* To handle roughly so as to cause injury. We chased the cat away before it could **maul** the mouse it had caught.
participate pär tis´ ə pāt	*v.* To take part in. The entire class **participated** in the ticket sale for the school musical. **participant** *n.* (pär tis´ ə pənt) One who takes part in. All the **participants** in the Thanksgiving Day parade must be in place by 11:00 a.m.
robust rō bust´	*adj.* Strong and vigorous. My grandfather is in **robust** health for an eighty-year-old.

19A Finding Meanings

Choose two phrases to form a sentence that correctly uses a word from Word List 19. Then write the sentence.

1. (a) that is difficult and exhausting. (c) that requires much preparation.
   (b) An alternative exercise is one   (d) A grueling exercise is one

   _____

   _____

2. (a) Distinction is   (c) the ability to put up with hardship.
   (b) Endurance is   (d) the ability to understand.

   _____

   _____

3. (a) A desolate road is   (c) one that is presented as a choice.
   (b) An alternative road is   (d) one that is very windy.

   _____

   _____

4. (a) show harm done.
   (b) Fluctuating results
   (c) Adverse results
   (d) follow one another in proper order.

   _____

5. (a) A desolate person is one who
   (b) A robust person is one who
   (c) is in poor health.
   (d) is filled with sorrow.

   _____

6. (a) To participate is to
   (b) move up and down.
   (c) act without thinking.
   (d) To fluctuate is to

   _____

7. (a) A dispatch is
   (b) a possible course of action.
   (c) a quickly sent message.
   (d) A distinction is

   _____

8. (a) Consecutive tests
   (b) fail to show a definite result.
   (c) Compulsory tests
   (d) follow one another without a break.

   _____

9. (a) a member of the dog family.
   (b) A canine is
   (c) an injury caused by a bite or scratch.
   (d) A participant is

   _____

10. (a) An aloof person is one who
    (b) A robust person is one who
    (c) stands apart from the rest.
    (d) is without hope.

    _____

Just the Right Word

Replace each phrase in bold with a single word (or form of the word) from the word list.

1. The woods are dark and **without a sign of life.**

2. Only persons who are extremely **strong and vigorous** should do these aerobic exercises.

3. Were you one of the **ones taking part** in the 100-meter dash?

4. Wearing seat belts is **required by law** in many states.

5. The trainer was rushed to the hospital when the tiger **attacked him and caused serious injuries to** his left arm and shoulder.

6. The judge **quickly put an end to** the case with an abrupt "These charges should never have been filed."

7. I walked home because the only **other choice open to me** was to wait two hours for the next bus.

8. Did they make any **attempt to show the difference** between what is real and what is imaginary?

9. We learned to **put up with** the long, cold winter season after we moved to Alaska.

10. The reviews were so **negative and damaging** that the play closed in a week.

adverse
aloof
alternative
canine
compulsory
consecutive
desolate
dispatch
distinction
endure
fluctuate
grueling
maul
participate
robust

Applying Meanings

Circle the letter or letters next to each correct answer. There may be more than one correct answer.

1. Which of the following belongs to the **canine** family?
   - (a) a wolf
   - (b) a puppy
   - (c) a poodle
   - (d) a hound

2. In which of the following can all people **participate?**
   - (a) major-league baseball
   - (b) a recycling program
   - (c) July 4th celebrations
   - (d) a fund-raising drive

3. Which of the following might show **fluctuations?**
   - (a) the price of gasoline
   - (b) the demand for oil
   - (c) the moon's orbit
   - (d) the distance from Seattle to Miami

4. Which of the following run **consecutively?**
   - (a) 1999, 2000, 2001
   - (b) 9, 11, 12, 10
   - (c) May, June, July
   - (d) Monday, Wednesday, Friday

5. Which of the following might be described as **desolate?**
   - (a) a deserted village
   - (b) a congested highway
   - (c) a solitary person
   - (d) an evicted family

6. Which of the following might be a **grueling** activity?
   - (a) running a marathon
   - (b) long-distance swimming
   - (c) watching a movie
   - (d) reading a book

7. Which of the following would be described as **compulsory** in the United States?
   - (a) voting in elections
   - (b) exercising regularly
   - (c) eating balanced meals
   - (d) paying any taxes owed

8. Which of the following could be **dispatched?**
   - (a) a letter
   - (b) a task
   - (c) a messenger
   - (d) a predatory animal

Word Study: Synonyms and Antonyms

Each group of four words contains either two synonyms or two antonyms. Circle that pair. Then circle the *S* if they are synonyms or the *A* if they are antonyms.

1.	feeble	desolate	beneficial	robust	S	A
2.	dispatch	caress	maul	decide	S	A
3.	endure	invent	participate	last	S	A
4.	excellence	alternative	change	distinction	S	A
5.	fluctuation	dispatch	hardiness	speed	S	A
6.	joy	wisdom	desolation	fluctuation	S	A
7.	friendly	grueling	afraid	aloof	S	A
8.	compulsory	advanced	adverse	favorable	S	A
9.	option	participant	alternative	hardship	S	A
10.	arduous	delicious	grueling	robust	S	A

adverse
aloof
alternative
canine
compulsory
consecutive
desolate
dispatch
distinction
endure
fluctuate
grueling
maul
participate
robust

The Ultimate Test

Most sports have separate divisions for men and women. No such **distinction** exists between male and female **participants** in the Iditarod, a **grueling** race of sixty or more dogsleds across 1,157 miles from Anchorage to Nome, Alaska. Probably its most famous competitor was Susan Butcher, who won the event for the third **consecutive** year in 1988, and who—despite the most **adverse** weather conditions in the history of the race—went on to win it for a fourth time in 1990. Butcher considered the Iditarod to be the ultimate test of **endurance** for both animals and humans.

The race, which extends over some of the most **desolate** trails on earth, lasts up to fourteen days. The competitors, called "mushers," get little sleep during this time. A **compulsory** twenty-four-hour stopover at the checkpoint of their choice gives them a brief respite. But even the most **robust** mushers have to fight a constant battle with fatigue during the race's final days.

Unpredictable weather conditions are another hazard. Temperatures can **fluctuate** between fifty degrees below zero and forty degrees above. Snowstorms are not uncommon, with icy winds reaching speeds of 140 miles an hour. In the 1984 race, a section of the overland route was closed. Strong winds had blown away the snow covering. Butcher and her dogs took an **alternative** sea route over the ice-covered Norton Sound. The ice gave way. Susan and her dog team plunged into the frigid water. Led by Granite, her lead dog, they scrambled for shore and went on with the race. Butcher stayed warm by running alongside her sled. That year she came in second.

Wild animals are another of the many dangers mushers face. In the 1985 race, Butcher's dog team was attacked by a starving moose that probably thought her dogs were a pack of wolves. Having to protect her dogs and herself, she fought off the enraged moose with an ax. Finally another musher, who was armed with a gun, pulled up behind her and quickly **dispatched** the moose. Two of her dogs were killed in the attack. Thirteen other dogs were badly **mauled.** That was one year she did not finish.

Born in 1954, Butcher had loved dogs since her youth. In 1975, she moved from her native Cambridge, Massachusetts, to Eureka, Alaska. There she bred and trained dogs at her Trail Breaker Kennels up until her death from leukemia in 2006. As many as 150 dogs were there at any one time. She said that they were all her pets and had the run of her home, although of course not all at once. Butcher was somewhat **aloof** by nature. She was more at ease with her dogs than she was with people. She believed that the secret of her success was the strong bond she formed with her **canine** companions from the time they were born.

As to the future of the Iditarod, Mother Nature and the effects of climate change have the final word. At the 2016 Iditarod, snow had to be brought in by train to provide enough cover for the race to take place.

▶ **Answer each of the following questions with a sentence. If a question does not contain a vocabulary word from the lesson's word list, use one in your answer. Use each word only once.**

1. What does the phrase "**adverse** weather conditions" suggest in the passage?

_____

_____

2. Do temperatures generally remain steady during the course of the Iditarod?

_____

_____

3. What are two qualities needed for success in such a **grueling** event?

_____

_____

4. What is the meaning of **desolate** as it is used in the passage?

_____

_____

5. What do the dogsled teams do if the route ahead is closed?

_____

_____

6. Is the twenty-four-hour stopover voluntary?

_____

_____

7. What is the meaning of **dispatched** as it is used in the passage?

_____

_____

| adverse |
| aloof |
| alternative |
| canine |
| compulsory |
| consecutive |
| desolate |
| dispatch |
| distinction |
| endure |
| fluctuate |
| grueling |
| maul |
| participate |
| robust |

8. Is fatigue a problem during the race's final days?

_____

_____

9. How many of Butcher's dogs were injured when the moose attacked?

_____

_____

10. Why do you think the moose mistook Butcher's dogs for wolves?

_____

_____

11. What does it mean to say that Butcher won for the third **consecutive** year in 1988?

_____

_____

12. Why might the start of the race be particularly hectic?

_____

_____

13. How is the Iditarod different from most athletic contests?

_____

_____

14. Why do you think so many people—like Butcher—respond to the challenge of the Iditarod?

_____

_____

15. Why might Butcher not have enjoyed going to parties?

_____

_____

Fun & Fascinating FACTS

- **Adverse** should not be confused with *averse*, which means "having an active, strong dislike." If a person has a serious heart condition, strenuous exercise might have an *adverse* effect on that person's health; such a person might, therefore, be *averse* to such exercise.

- Don't confuse **alternative** (the noun or the adjective) with *alternate*, the verb meaning "to happen by turns" or "to take turns." (Boys and girls *alternate* in using the swimming pool.) *Alternate* is also an adjective, meaning "happening by turns" (The wall was painted in *alternate* stripes of red and white) and "every other" (We take turns driving the children on *alternate* days). Finally, *alternate* is a noun meaning "a person chosen to take the place of another." (If you cannot attend the meeting, you must name an *alternate*.)

- **Canine** comes from the Latin word for *dog*, which is *canis*.

Latin names of other animals provide us with a number of words having to do with animals or with qualities associated with them. Among them are the following: *Apis*, "bee," gives us *apiary*, a collection of hives where bees are kept for their honey. *Avis*, "bird," gives us *aviary*, a large, caged enclosure where birds are kept, and *aviation*, which is the science of airplanes and flying. *Asinus*, "donkey," gives us *asinine*, which means "like a donkey" and, hence, "stupid" or "silly" because of the old belief that donkeys are stupid animals.

adverse
aloof
alternative
canine
compulsory
consecutive
desolate
dispatch
distinction
endure
fluctuate
grueling
maul
participate
robust

fluctuate

verb To rise and fall; to keep changing.

Academic Context

In science, you learn how changes to the climate in a region, such as when the temperature **fluctuates,** can affect the populations of certain plants and animals.

Discussion & Writing Prompt

Describe how you would be affected if the outside temperature **fluctuated** from very high on one day to very low on the next day.

2 min.	3 min.
1. Turn and talk to your partner or group.	2. Write 2–4 sentences.
Use this space to take notes or draw your ideas.	Be ready to share what you have written.

Study the definitions of the words. Then do the exercises that follow.

apathy
ap´ ə thē

n. A lack of interest or concern.
I feel nothing but **apathy** when it comes to sports.

apathetic *adj.* (ap ə thet´ ik) Unconcerned; uninterested.
Some teenagers remain **apathetic** about politics until they can vote.

Tell your partner something you are apathetic about, such as the weather or cooking.

badger
baj´ ər

v. To keep bothering.
She kept **badgering** her parents until they let her go to the party.

n. A strongly built, burrowing mammal common in many northern parts of the world.
The European **badger** weighs up to thirty pounds and is somewhat larger than its North American counterpart.

Badger your partner to tell you something you don't know about him or her.

compel
kəm pel´

v. To force or require to do something.
A strong sense of duty **compels** firefighters to risk their lives.

delude
də lōōd´

v. To mislead; to deceive.
Despite never having practiced the long jump in track, Emmanuel **deluded** himself into thinking he could win.

delusion *n.* (də lōō´ zhən) A false or mistaken belief.
His belief that he is Napoleon is a **delusion.**

deplore
di plôr´

v. 1. To feel or express sorrow or regret.
My father **deplored** the fact that he hadn't spent more time with his children when they were young.

2. To disapprove of strongly.
Graciela **deplored** the way some students picked on the smallest person in the class.

deplorable *adj.* Very bad; wretched.
Living conditions in the small village were **deplorable.**

Share with your partner a behavior you deplore, such as littering.

derelict
der´ ə likt

adj. 1. Dilapidated and abandoned.
The **derelict** building will be torn down soon.

2. Lacking a sense of duty; neglectful.
The teacher was **derelict** in her duty to take attendance every day.

n. A poor, homeless person.
The plan will help **derelicts** by providing shelters.

detriment
de´ trə mənt

n. 1. Damage or harm.
She willingly stayed home with her young children to the **detriment** of her career.

2. Anything that causes harm.
Lack of exercise is a **detriment** to the health of people of all ages.

detrimental *adj.* Damaging; harmful.
Eating too much junk food is **detrimental** to one's health.

Talk to your partner about the detrimental effects of not getting enough sleep.

diversity
də vʉr´ sə tē

n. 1. The condition of being different or having differences.
I was struck by the **diversity** in the personalities of the twins.

2. Variety.
The library offers a great **diversity** of materials on local history.

Discuss with your partner the best part of living in an area where there is population diversity.

emit
ē mit´

v. 1. To give off or send out.
A candle **emits** very little light.

2. To utter or express.
The cat **emitted** a loud screech when I accidentally stepped on its tail.

emission *n.* (ē mish´ ən) Something that is emitted.
Carbon monoxide is an odorless yet deadly **emission** from engine exhausts.

foster
fôs´ tər

v. To promote the growth of; to encourage.
The music teacher **fostered** an interest in jazz in her students.

adj. Giving or receiving care in a family that is not related by birth or adoption.
The Becks are **foster** parents to three small children.

inanimate
in an´ ə mət

adj. Lacking qualities associated with living things.
A stone is an **inanimate** object.

With your partner, quickly make a list of ten inanimate objects in the classroom.

	n. Something that makes a person want to try or work harder.
incentive in sen´ tiv	A local benefactor offers $1,000 scholarships as an **incentive** to students to stay in school.

	n. An event or sign that is believed to indicate the future.
omen ō´ mən	Do you believe that a black cat is an **omen** of bad luck?
	ominous *adj.* (äm´ ə nəs) Of or like a bad omen; threatening. An **ominous** silence greeted us when we entered the room.

Chat with your partner about what it means when there is a dark, ominous sky.

	n. A group of plants or animals that are similar in some ways.
species spē´ shēz	There are over a million different **species** of beetle in the world.

	adj. Causing harm; poisonous.
toxic täks´ ik	Pokeweed can be **toxic** to birds that eat its seeds.

20A Using Words in Context

Read the following sentences. If the word in bold is used correctly, write C on the line. If the word is used incorrectly, write I on the line.

apathy
badger
compel
delude
deplore
derelict
detriment
diversity
emit
foster
inanimate
incentive
omen
species
toxic

1. (a) I **deplored** my parents to let me go on the trip with my friend. ___
   (b) The **deplorable** sound of children laughing always cheers me up. ___
   (c) We **deplore** the horrible way you were treated. ___
   (d) The **deplorable** food in the cafeteria must be changed. ___

2. (a) The **apathy** of the voters resulted in a low turnout. ___
   (b) The **apathetic** response to my request for help left me frustrated. ___
   (c) The **apathetic** looks on their faces told me they wanted to know more. ___
   (d) The **apathy** in my bones makes me ache in the morning. ___

3. (a) The smoke alarm **emits** a signal every few minutes. ___
   (b) My mother **emitted** a sigh of relief when the doctor said my leg wasn't broken. ___
   (c) Experts monitored harmful **emissions** from cars. ___
   (d) I **emitted** several names off the list of people who weren't qualified. ___

4. (a) Our trip was **deluded** over an hour because of a problem with the car. ___
   (b) Angela was **deluded** into thinking she had magical powers. ___
   (c) Reports of unicorns are **delusions** and can be ignored. ___
   (d) We were **deluded** to hear that we were among the finalists. ___

5. (a) A comet in the night sky was considered an **omen** by the ancient tribe. ___
   (b) **Ominous** black clouds on the horizon threatened stormy weather. ___
   (c) The **omen** was found deep in the earth under the garage. ___
   (d) I kept an **omen** with me and rubbed it for good luck. ___

6. (a) Voters in Australia are **compelled** by law to vote. ___
   (b) I **compelled** the two sandwiches and then made my choice. ___
   (c) What **compels** a person to climb Mount Everest? ___
   (d) The diamond is **compelled** between two rubies in the necklace. ___

7. (a) I put salt and pepper on the table, along with the other **detriments.** ___
   (b) Aidan spent the evening playing video games, to the **detriment** of his test score the next day. ___
   (c) Traces of lead in the drinking water have a **detrimental** effect on health. ___
   (d) The **detriment** is taken away and disposed of safely. ___

8. (a) Aarón's class hamster was full of **diversity.** ___
   (b) Colleges promote **diversity** in their advertising materials. ___
   (c) The store offers a **diversity** of products. ___
   (d) Ellen dove off the **diversity** and into the pool. ___

9. (a) A pencil is an **inanimate** object. ___
   (b) Nizhoni and Polly had been **inanimate** friends since childhood. ___
   (c) Cyrus becomes **inanimate** as he flies across the field during a game. ___
   (d) **Inanimate** crystals sparkled in the cave. ___

10. (a) We **foster** an interest in reading by providing free books. ___
    (b) There is a need for **foster** parents in the community. ___
    (c) We **foster** the growth of crops by adding fertilizer. ___
    (d) Several new names were **fostered** to the list. ___

20B Making Connections

Circle the letter next to each correct answer. There may be more than one correct answer.

1. Which word or words go with *annoy?*
   (a) exasperate   (b) emit   (c) badger   (d) harass

2. Which word or words go with *careless?*
   (a) lax   (b) inanimate   (c) derelict   (d) incentive

3. Which word or words go with *reward?*
   (a) detriment   (b) emission   (c) incentive   (d) theme

4. Which word or words go with *variety?*
   (a) prospective   (b) blithe   (c) emission   (d) diversity

5. Which word or words go with *deadly?*
   (a) apathetic   (b) lethal   (c) toxic   (d) fatal

6. Which word or words go with *threatening?*
   (a) apathetic   (b) ominous   (c) sinister   (d) dismal

7. Which word or words go with *unreal?*
   (a) figment   (b) delusion   (c) species   (d) incentive

8. Which word or words go with *uninterested?*
   (a) toxic   (b) apathetic   (c) indifferent   (d) deplorable

9. Which word or words go with *harmful?*
   (a) concise   (b) formidable   (c) detrimental   (d) prospective

10. Which word or words go with *disapprove?*
   (a) deplore   (b) foster   (c) denounce   (d) emit

| apathy |
| badger |
| compel |
| delude |
| deplore |
| derelict |
| detriment |
| diversity |
| emit |
| foster |
| inanimate |
| incentive |
| omen |
| species |
| toxic |

Determining Meanings

Circle the letter next to each answer choice that correctly completes the sentence. There may be more than one correct answer.

1. The **toxicity**
   (a) of too much carbon monoxide is well known.
   (b) that Hamid gave me burst into color.
   (c) in the lightbulb shone brightly.
   (d) of the substance may cause death.

2. Each **species**
   (a) occupies its own place in the plant and animal kingdoms.
   (b) is unique in its ability to remain alive.
   (c) of building has its own theme.
   (d) of classroom has its own teaching assistant.

3. An **incentive**
   (a) came up with the idea of skipping classes.
   (b) is the same thing as an empty mailbox.
   (c) was given to reward the team if they played well during the big game.
   (d) to help came in the form of money.

4. **Inanimate**
   (a) creatures like the great apes are fast becoming extinct.
   (b) objects can be mistaken for living things in the dim light.
   (c) layers of rock have much to tell us about history.
   (d) looks were exchanged between the two sisters.

5. To **emit**
   (a) smoke signals is one way to communicate.
   (b) that she was wrong could not have been easy for Shakira.
   (c) students under eighteen to the club is illegal.
   (d) light, the lamp must be turned on.

6. **Derelict**
   (a) coins, three thousand years old and in excellent condition, have been discovered.
   (b) in her chaperone duties, the teacher did not prevent the accident.
   (c) new homes were recently built along the river.
   (d) parts of town are in need of help.

7. What **compels**

    (a) Olympic athletes to compete at such a high level?

    (b) people to make the same mistake over and over?

    (c) a submarine as it moves underwater?

    (d) mild weather into a hurricane in just three days?

8. Don't **badger**

    (a) the librarian with silly questions.

    (b) the job and then try to blame someone else.

    (c) the server with complaints about the food.

    (d) yourself into a corner that you can't easily get out of.

20D Completing Sentences

Complete the sentences to demonstrate your knowledge of the words in bold.

apathy
badger
compel
delude
deplore
derelict
detriment
diversity
emit
foster
inanimate
incentive
omen
species
toxic

1. My favorite **species** is

    _____ .

2. One example of an **omen** of bad luck is

    _____ .

3. **Diversity** is important because

    _____ .

4. I would like to **foster** in other people

    _____ .

5. A habit that is **detrimental** to our health is

    _____ .

6. One thing I **deplore** is

    _____ .

7. It is a **delusion** to think that

    _____ .

8. To feel **apathy** means

    _____ .

9. An **incentive** to do my homework is

    _____ .

10. If you **compel** someone to do something, that means

    _____ .

Saving the Planet

Smog is a mixture of smoke and fog. Americans became unhappily aware of it in the 1960s when it hung over Los Angeles for days on end. Smog made the air not only unpleasant to breathe but actually **detrimental** to people's health. Many believed this polluted air, produced by smoke from vehicle exhausts and factory chimneys, to be an **omen** of things to come if people did not take better care of the environment.

The environment is the world we inhabit—everything living and **inanimate.** Environmentalists are people who wish to preserve the environment; they **deplore** the damage we are doing to it and remind us that we share our planet with millions of other **species** of plants and animals. They cherish this **diversity** of life and believe we all should do the same.

For a long time, governments, at both the state and national level, had been **derelict** when it came to protecting the environment. The chief reason for this was the **apathy** of the public. The public was largely unaware of environmental damage until it was almost too late. Rachel Carson's *Silent Spring*, published in 1962, warned of the harm being done to the environment by overuse of chemical fertilizers and pesticides. Her book had an enormous impact. Voters began to take an interest in environmental issues. That gave lawmakers the **incentive** to take action. Environmentalists **badgered** Congress to pass laws such as the Clean Air Acts of 1970 and 1990. Finally, industries that were the worst polluters were **compelled** to reduce the **emissions** from vehicles and factory chimneys.

Citizens cannot, however, be **deluded** into thinking that simply passing laws will protect people from environmental harm. Individuals must remain active. An example of a person who did just this is Janice Dickerson. She made it her mission in life to educate people about the dangers of living along a seventy-five-mile stretch of the Mississippi River south of Baton Rouge, Louisiana. During recent decades, the area witnessed the building of more than one hundred chemical factories and oil refineries. Those factories emitted smoke from chimneys and dumped chemicals into the river. Known as "cancer alley," this area has one of the highest cancer rates in the United States.

One evening in March 2015, LeeAnne Walters, of Flint, Michigan, decided she had had enough. Her family had been suffering from numerous medical problems for months. Her twin sons kept breaking out in rashes, and one had stopped growing normally. Others in her family had been rushed to the hospital with stomach problems. But that March evening was when LeeAnne decided to act. That was when her eldest daughter showed her a clump of hair that had fallen out while she was taking a shower.

LeeAnne Walters suspected that something in the drinking water might be the cause. She sent a sample to the Environmental Protection Agency (EPA), where it was tested and found to contain high levels of lead, one of the most **toxic** substances known. LeeAnne, working closely with the EPA, discovered the cause. To save money, the city had switched its drinking-supply water from Lake Huron to the Flint River, a former dumping ground for manufacturers. Other nearby towns tested their water and found that the problem was more widespread than Flint. The cost to replace water pipes will run into billions of dollars.

One of the most effective ways of getting people involved in environmental issues has been Earth Day. The purpose of Earth Day is to **foster** awareness of the harm we are doing to our planet. Started in 1970 in the United States, it has grown rapidly, and on Earth Day in 2009, more than a billion people around the world participated in its activities. Earth Day is celebrated each year on April 22, but to those who care about the environment, every day is Earth Day.

| apathy |
| badger |
| compel |
| delude |
| deplore |
| derelict |
| detriment |
| diversity |
| emit |
| foster |
| inanimate |
| incentive |
| omen |
| species |
| toxic |

▶ **Answer each of the following questions with a sentence. If a question does not contain a vocabulary word from the lesson's word list, use one in your answer. Use each word only once.**

1. Is the environment composed only of living things?

_____

_____

2. How might your class **foster** awareness of Earth Day?

_____

_____

3. Why was it necessary to reduce smog in the nation's cities?

_____

_____

4. In terms of their future, what did people especially fear about smog?

_____

_____

5. Why were people concerned when lead was discovered in the water of Flint?

_____

_____

6. Were Dickerson and Walters content simply to **deplore** the harm being done to the environment?

_____

_____

7. How did Rachel Carson help end people's **apathy?**

_____

_____

8. What is the meaning of **derelict** as it is used in the passage?

_____

_____

9. Why did lawmakers wait until 1970 to pass the first Clean Air Act?

_____

_____

10. How did environmentalists influence Congress to do something about pollution?

_____

_____

11. What effect did laws such as the Clean Air Acts have on industry?

_____

_____

12. What was the main cause of the smog in Los Angeles in the 1960s?

_____

_____

13. Does the passage say that simply passing laws will protect people from environmental harm?

_____

_____

14. What does every human being have in common with every other human?

_____

_____

15. Why do environmentalists wish to preserve the environment?

_____

_____

Fun & Fascinating FACTS

- The Greek word *pathos* means "suffering" or "feeling" and has passed unchanged into English; *pathos* in English means "something that moves a person to feel pity." The Greek prefix *ab-* (sometimes written *a-*) means "not" or "without" and combines with *pathos* to form the word **apathy.** A person who cannot feel for others or who doesn't care about them is in a state of *apathy.* We say that such a person is *apathetic.*

  The Greek prefix *syn-* (sometimes written *sym-*) means "with" or "together." It combines with *pathos* to form the noun *sympathy,* "an emotional feeling for other people and a sharing of their sorrow." The adjective form is *sympathetic.* If you have a serious problem, you need to talk to someone who is *sympathetic.* Someone who is *apathetic* would not be interested in your problem.

- Don't confuse **emit,** which means "to give off," with *omit,* which means "to leave out."

- **Species** is both a singular noun (a *species*) and a plural noun (many *species*). A species is one of the major groups into which all living things—plants and animals—are divided. Although the production of offspring normally takes place only within the same *species,* creatures of different, though related, *species* can produce offspring. An example of this is the mule; it is the result of mating a male donkey with a female horse.

  Specie (a less common word, spelled without the final *s*) means "money in the form of coin." Dollar bills are paper money. Nickels, dimes, and quarters are money in the form of *specie.*

apathy
badger
compel
delude
deplore
derelict
detriment
diversity
emit
foster
inanimate
incentive
omen
species
toxic

diversity

noun 1. The condition of being different or having differences.

2. A variety of different things, people, or ideas.

Academic Context

In science class, you learn how environmental factors contribute to the **diversity** of plant and animal life.

Word Family

diverse (adjective)

diversely (adverb)

diversification (noun)

diversified (adjective)

diversify (verb)

Discussion & Writing Prompt

If a community is culturally **diverse,** it contains a variety of social or ethnic groups. Think about your community. Does it have cultural **diversity?** Explain.

2 min.	3 min.
1. Turn and talk to your partner or group.	**2.** Write 2–4 sentences.
Use this space to take notes or draw your ideas.	Be ready to share what you have written.

Hidden Message   In the boxes provided, write the words from Lessons 17 through 20 that are missing in each of the sentences. The number after each sentence is the lesson the word is from. When the exercise is finished, the shaded boxes should spell out a Burma Shave jingle. From the 1920s to the 1960s, Burma Shave signs—a form of advertising for a shaving cream—were a familiar sight on American roads. On four or five regularly spaced signs, short messages were spelled out for travelers to read as they passed by. This one dates back to 1949.

1. Grain prices _____ greatly from year to year. **(19)**

2. The play's _____ is the healing power of love. **(18)**

3. Her parents admire their _____ son-in-law. **(18)**

4. I was surprised to hear him _____ such a generous offer. **(18)**

5. That row of _____ houses is to be torn down. **(20)**

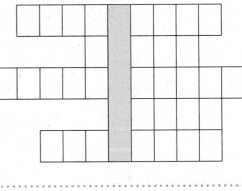

6. I am a(n) _____ supporter of the right to free speech. **(18)**

7. You might have to _____ to get a lower price. **(17)**

8. A(n) _____ country will not allow foreign interference. **(17)**

9. She continues to _____ herself into thinking that the job will be easy. **(20)**

10. The child was placed in the care of _____ parents. **(20)**

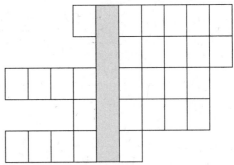

11. I think my brother will be _____ to my offer. **(17)**

12. The _____ of plant life in the rain forest is enormous. **(20)**

13. The last five miles of the marathon were _____. **(19)**

14. Why _____ the possessions of others? **(18)**

15. The curfew will _____ youths to be home by 1 a.m. **(20)**

16. You give your _____ to the plan by voting yes. **(17)**

17. Some mushrooms are _____, so they shouldn't be eaten. **(20)**

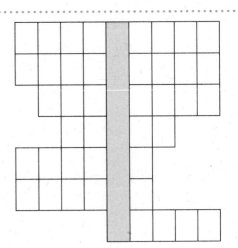

18. If you bother it, the bear may _____ you. **(19)**

19. The parents _____ with the club's decision to raise the dues. **(17)**

20. I tried to _____ her from leaving school. **(17)**

21. The family felt trapped in the inner city _____. **(18)**

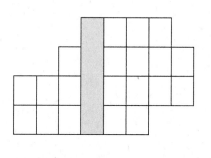

22. A(n) _____ handler looks after the dogs. **(19)**

23. We want everyone to _____ in the project. **(19)**

24. It rained last month for twelve _____ days. **(19)**

25. Raising a sunken ship is a(n) _____ task. **(18)**

26. An honest person will _____ a bribe. **(17)**

27. Acid rain has a(n) _____ affect on plant growth. **(19)**

28. She has the _____ of winning two Nobel prizes. **(19)**

29. Stars _____ light and other forms of energy. **(20)**

30. The _____ left a wife and one grown child. **(18)**

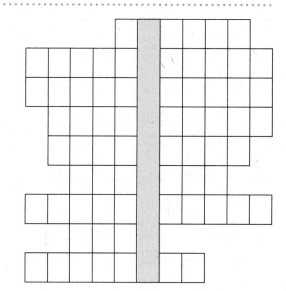

31. I do not _____ any difference between them. **(18)**

32. He preferred to stay _____ from the crowd. **(19)**

33. It is _____ to have a parent sign your homework. **(19)**

34. I managed to _____ some extra supplies. **(17)**

35. His continued absence began to _____ me. **(17)**

36. It is in the nature of dictators to _____ the people. **(18)**

37. Even at ninety, her health remained _____. **(19)**

38. Some people don't vote because of _____. **(20)**

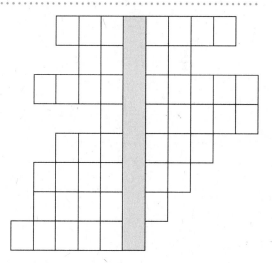

39. The medical breakthrough won national _____. **(18)**

40. They'll _____ him until he changes his mind. **(20)**

41. The music of Mozart will _____ forever. **(19)**

42. The _____ of their neighbors made the newcomers uncomfortable. **(18)**

43. Rocks, cars, and planets are all _____ objects. **(20)**

44. We _____ violence in all its forms. **(20)**

45. There is a(n) _____ route into town. **(19)**

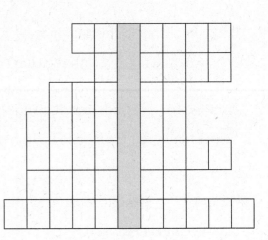

46. Lions and tigers belong to different _____. **(20)**

47. The president _____ federal judges. **(17)**

48. Not exercising is _____ to one's health. **(20)**

49. The _____ of her new play is tomorrow night. **(18)**

50. Antarctica is the most _____ place on earth. **(19)**

51. The + sign is used to _____ addition. **(17)**

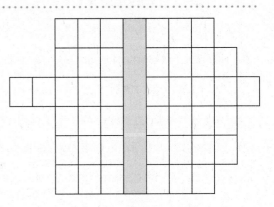

52. We will _____ a repair crew at once to fix the furnace. **(19)**

53. A red sunset is said to be a(n) _____ of good weather. **(20)**

54. The fall of Rome was a(n) _____ event in world history. **(18)**

55. You should _____ your doctor if the pain worsens. **(17)**

56. Joining the orchestra was her _____ for practicing so many hours. **(20)**

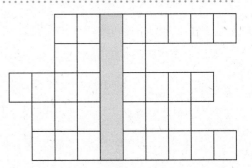

Pronunciation Key

Symbol	Key Words	Symbol	Key Words
a	cat	b	bed
ā	ape	d	dog
ä	cot, car	f	fall
â	bear	g	get
		h	help
e	ten, berry	j	jump
ē	me	k	kiss, call
		l	leg, bottle
i	fit	m	meat
ī	ice, fire	n	nose, kitten
		p	put
ō	go	r	red
ô	fall, for	s	see
oi	oil	t	top
o͝o	look, pull	v	vat
o͞o	tool, rule	w	wish
ou	out, crowd	y	yard
		z	zebra
u	up		
ʉ	fur, shirt	ch	chin, arch
		ŋ	ring, drink
ə	a in ago	sh	she, push
	e in agent	th	thin, truth
	i in pencil	*th*	then, father
	o in atom	zh	measure
	u in circus		

A stress mark ´ is placed after a syllable that gets a primary stress, as in **vocabulary** (vō kab´ yə ler ē).